Lecture Notes in Computer Science   4147

Commenced Publication in 1973
Founding and Former Series Editors:
Gerhard Goos, Juris Hartmanis, and Jan van Leeuw

T0238226

Editorial Board

Manfred Broy   Ingolf H. Krüger
Michael Meisinger (Eds.)

Automotive Software –
Connected Services
in Mobile Networks

First Automotive Software Workshop, ASWSD 2004
San Diego, CA, USA, January 10-12, 2004
Revised Selected Papers

 Springer

Volume Editors

Manfred Broy
Institut für Informatik
Technische Universität München
Boltzmannstr. 3
D-85748 Garching, Germany
E-mail: broy@informatik.tu-muenchen.de

Ingolf H. Krüger
University of California, San Diego
Computer Science and Engineering
9500 Gilman Drive
La Jolla, CA 92093-0404, USA
E-mail: ikrueger@cs.ucsd.edu

Michael Meisinger
Institut für Informatik
Technische Universität München
Boltzmannstr. 3
D-85748 Garching, Germany
E-mail: meisinge@informatik.tu-muenchen.de

Library of Congress Control Number: 2006932846

CR Subject Classification (1998): C.2.4, C.3, C.4, C.5.3, D.1.3, D.2.1, D.2.2, D.2.3, D.2.4, D.2.7, D.2.11, D.2.12, D.2.13, D.3.1, D.4, H.3-5, J.7

LNCS Sublibrary: SL 3 – Information Systems and Application, incl. Internet/Web and HCI

ISSN   0302-9743
ISBN-10   3-540-37677-1 Springer Berlin Heidelberg New York
ISBN-13   978-3-540-37677-4 Springer Berlin Heidelberg New York

Springer is a part of Springer Science+Business Media

springer.com

© Springer-Verlag Berlin Heidelberg 2006
Printed in Germany

Typesetting: Camera-ready by author, data conversion by Scientific Publishing Services, Chennai, India
Printed on acid-free paper   SPIN: 11823063   06/3142   5 4 3 2 1 0

Preface

Software development for the automotive domain is currently subject to a silent revolution. On the one hand, software has become the enabling technology for almost all safety-critical and comfort functions offered to the customer. A total of 90 % of all innovations in automotive systems are directly or indirectly enabled by software. Today's luxury cars contain up to 80 electronic control units (ECUs) and 5 different, inter-connected network platforms, over which some 700 software-enabled functions are distributed.

On the other hand, the complexity induced by this large number of functions, their interactions, and their supporting infrastructure has started to become *the* limiting factor for automotive software development. Adequate management of this complexity is particularly important; the following list highlights three of the corresponding challenges:

First, the dependencies between safety-critical and comfort functions are rapidly increasing; a simple example is the interplay of airbag control and power seat control in the case of an accident. Careful analysis and design of these dependencies are necessary to yield correct software solutions.

Second, advances in wired and wireless networking infrastructures enable interconnection between cars and backend service providers (e.g., to call for help in cases of emergency), between cars and devices brought into the car by drivers and passengers (such as cell phones, PDAs, and laptops), and even among cars. This dramatically shifts the focus from the development of individual software solutions residing on dedicated ECUs to their distribution and interaction within and beyond car boundaries.

Third, the myriad of functions and services offered to the driver and passengers need to be effectively accessible without compromising traffic safety. This requires user interfaces addressing not only ease of use but also priority of information necessary for safe vehicle operation, and choice of interface modality (e.g., voice versus pushing of buttons for menu selection) for reasons of adequacy or user limitations.

These challenges are aggravated by demanding time-to-market requirements, short development cycles, rapid change of technological infrastructures, customer demands, and product lines. The silent revolution currently underway in the automotive domain thus consists of a shift of focus from hardware to software infrastructures and from ECUs to software services as the center of concern in the development process. This puts the *software architecture* for future generation automotive systems in the spotlight as a critical element both for enabling advanced services supporting drivers and passengers, and for managing the complexity of these functions amidst the high safety demands they are subject to.

The goal for the first Automotive Software Workshop, San Diego, ASWSD 2004, was to bring together experts from industry and academia, who work on highly complex, distributed, reactive software systems related to the automotive domain, and to discuss and further the understanding of the following focus areas:

- Automotive Software and Software Architectures
- Automotive Domain Architectures
- Automotive Software Services
- Automotive Hardware, Middleware, and Software Platforms
- On- and Off-Board Ad-Hoc Networking
- Networked Automotive Services
- Mobile Sensor Networks
- Reliability, Security and Privacy for Automotive Software
- Enabling Technologies for Telematics Applications

The workshop, which took place during January 10–12, 2004 in La Jolla, CA, USA, contributed to fostering a deeper understanding of the research challenges and agendas in this area. Potentials for cross-disciplinary research, as well as pertinent curricula and training programs to address these challenges were identified and discussed.

The workshop program consisted of 4 keynote presentations, 22 technical paper presentations and 2 panel discussions. The workshop spanned two-and-a-half days and was divided into the following topical sessions: Quality Assurance (QA), Networking Infrastructures and Applications (NI), Real-Time Control (RT), Services and Components (SC), and Model-Based Development and Tools (MD). The pre-proceedings, consisting of the presentation slide sets, were made available at *http://aswsd.ucsd.edu/2004*.

To foster discussion on cross-cutting and interdisciplinary topics the organizers decided to have four keynote presentations (two from industry and two from academia) and two panel discussions as integral parts of the workshop program. Hans-Georg Frischkorn (then BMW Group), Hermann Kopetz (TU Vienna), K. Venkatesh Prasad (Ford Motor Company), and Janos Sztipanovits (Vanderbilt University) were recruited as keynote speakers. Professor Larry Smarr (Director, Calit2) delivered opening remarks on the first day of the workshop.

Hans-Georg Frischkorn (then Senior Vice President System Architecture and System Integration, BMW Group) delivered the opening keynote "Automotive Software – The Silent Revolution" in the Quality Assurance session, where he laid out BMW's automotive software vision to realize innovative software-based functionality in cars. He stressed the importance of software architectures and infrastructures, and promoted an open software platform providing extensibility, updatability and support for easy integration of new functionality. Frischkorn showed how the tasks of operating and maintaining future vehicle generations could be supported by system services provided on multiple layers of abstraction.

The keynote presentation for the session on Real-Time Control was given by *Hermann Kopetz* (Technical University of Vienna); he stressed the importance of having a fault-hypothesis for safety-critical real-time systems. Kopetz concluded that (a) the design of safety-critical computing systems requires a fault-tolerant architecture and a rigorous design methodology, (b) the precise specification of the fault hypothesis is the key document in the design of fault-tolerant systems, and (c) the architecture of a safety critical application must tolerate the arbitrary failure of any single VLSI chip since one cannot assume that a chip contains two independent fault containment regions.

The Services and Components session started with the keynote by *K. Venkatesh Prasad* (Leader Ford Motor Company's Infotronics Technologies Group). He sketched the future of automotive product creation, involving the rapid convergence of enterprise and embedded computing and of portable-mobile, fixed-mobile and fixed wireless communications. Prasad argued that creating an automobile clearly calls for a series of innovations that in turn rely on a body of inventions, literature and competencies that are created and nurtured in academia and the broad industrial and public sector research & development base. This highlighted the emerging role of software technologies and processes in modern automotive product creation, and stimulated thinking in terms of how academic curricula might need to evolve and what types of new collaboration styles might be needed for the creation of sustainable mobility solutions in the future.

Janos Sztipanovits (Vanderbilt Univeristy) delivered the keynote speech, titled "Model-Integrated Computing", for the session on Model-Based Development, and Tools. Sztipanovits pointed out that despite it being a seemingly simple concept, building large systems from components is a very hard problem. In particular, the side-effects of component composition as manifested in component interactions often transpire only during system integration (compositionality problem), and the responsibility for design integrity lies with each system integrator (semantics problem). These problems are aggravated by physical requirements that cross-cut functional component-boundaries, and thus defy compositionality. Sztipanovits identified the following challenges for model-integrated computing: the creation and application of domain specific modeling languages (DSMLs), model synthesis, and model transformation. He then promoted the use of meta-modeling as a means for capturing the semantics of different target languages and execution models; he distinguished between domain models as capturing designs, and meta-models as capturing design invariants (such as types, constraints, and well-formedness rules). Sztipanovits also discussed the Generic Modeling Environment (GME), developed at Vanderbilt University, based on meta-modeling and model-transformation concepts. He concluded that domain-specific modeling languages and model-transformations are key technologies for future progress in embedded systems development, and that model-integrated computing is becoming a mature technology for the development of complex applications.

Two panel discussions complemented the keynote presentations. The first panel discussed "Research Challenges in Automotive Software" as well as the role of academia, industry and funding agencies in addressing these challenges. Panelists were *Hans-Georg Frischkorn* (then BMW Group), *K. Venkatesh Prasad* (Ford Motor Company), *Dev Kambhampati* (UC Discovery) and *Ramesh Rao* (California Institute for Telecommunications and Information Technology). Discussions emphasized the importance of software architectures in automotive software development and research, their integration into effective development processes, the availability of a defined middleware platform, the view of automotive software within broader system boundaries and the importance of user experience in the automotive design. The discussion also highlighted the need for an increased understanding of software as a product on the sides of both manufacturers and suppliers, the availability of business plans taking software into account, and access to engineers trained in system architecture and integration. Collaboration between industry and academia, as well as long-term fundamental research, is required to address these issues.

The second panel discussed "Challenges in Model-Based Design of Automotive Software". Panelists were *Werner Damm* (University of Oldenburg, Germany), *Edward C. Nelson* (Ford Motor Company), *Jürgen Bielefeld* (BMW Group) and *Carlo Ghezzi* (Politecnico di Milano, Italy). The discussion emphasized the importance of models that need to be kept consistent with software implementations and allow for incremental development and variant/product-line management. Models were also identified as a good means of communication between manufacturer and supplier. The importance of capturing system-wide views, such as the interactions of different system components, was also highlighted in the discussion. The utility of partial views, focused on separate services and addressing multiple levels of abstraction, was identified. Further research in developing modeling languages with thoroughly worked-out theories addressing the semantic level was suggested; a model repository was proposed as a valuable tool for the research community to compare modeling approaches and tools.

Selected Papers

This volume includes a selection of refereed technical and invited papers presented at the workshop. In the following we give a brief overview of the selected papers and their contents.

The contribution "Analyzing the Worst-Case Execution Time by Abstract Interpretation of Executable Code" by *Christian Ferdinand et al.*, addresses the validation of timing behaviors and memory usage as it occurs in embedded microprocessors by means of abstract interpretation of executable code.

In their paper "Quality Assurance and Certification of Software Modules in Safety Critical Automotive Electronic Control Units Using a CASE-Tool Integration Platform", *Klaus Müller-Glaser et al.* describe a CASE tool integration platform for quality assurance and certification of software modules.

In "On the Fault Hypothesis for a Safety-Critical Real-Time System", the paper accompanying his keynote presentation, *Hermann Kopetz* discusses the critical role of systematic failure management for systems prevalent in the automotive domain. This includes, in particular, the formulation of an explicit fault hypothesis, which has important consequences especially for the architecture design of safety-critical systems.

In "A Compositional Framework for Real-Time Guarantees", *Insup Lee et al.* describe a formal approach for establishing real-time properties for a composite system out of real-time properties for its parts.

Carlo Ghezzi et al. propose modeling component and service federations in "Validation of Component and Service Federations in Automotive Software Applications". Component federations can be modeled using statecharts (for individual components) and MSC variants (for interaction properties); service federations can be described using static architectural models, constraints on model transformations, and sequence diagrams for interaction properties.

The paper "Towards a Component Architecture for Hard Real Time Control Applications" by *Wolfgang Pree and Josef Templ* describes Giotto, a platform-independent, deterministic software model for embedded systems, with the goal of abstracting from the target hardware platform in the early development stages, and of supporting moving code modules from one ECU to another in the target system. One challenge addressed by Giotto is to specify timing-behavior independently from concrete scheduling algorithms and communication platforms.

In "Adding Value to Automotive Models", *Werner Damm et al.* describe advanced code-generation and validation techniques as a means for adding value to the models themselves. This can be accomplished by means of in-depth knowledge of the formal semantics behind the corresponding modeling tools, in-depth knowledge of the use of these tools, and extensive cooperation with the corresponding tool vendors.

Gabor Karsai, in "Automotive Software: A Challenge and Opportunity for Model-Based Software Development", identifies modeling and model-transformation as a common theme across the model-construction, analysis, and synthesis and integration phases of system development. According to Karsai, this makes the case for meta-programmable tools and corresponding tool-chains.

The paper "Software for Automotive Systems: Model-Integrated Computing" by *Sandeep Neema et al.* presents an exemplary design flow for automotive system development based on the Generic Modeling Environment (GME) and tool connectors for Simulink/Stateflow, Matlab, and specific code generators for the target platform.

Finally, in "Simulink Integration of Giotto/TDL", *Wolfgang Pree et al.* report on a case study carried out together with BMW on a throttle control; in this case study, the executable code was generated fully automatically from specifications of both the timing and the functional model. Using specialized translators the properties as specified in Simulink were transformed and simulated within a dedicated tool-set.

Outcome

The workshop clearly exhibited the state-of-the-art of automotive software engineering and pointed out various challenges in the area. This is also reflected by the papers selected for this volume. In particular, the idea of the workshop to bring together leading engineers from the Automotive domain with key researchers on an international level also stimulating the discussion between Europe and the US proved to be very fruitful and worked out perfectly. During the workshop significant progress was achieved towards developing a common understanding of the challenging problems in the automotive domain such as:

- standards for architectures and ways of structuring software systems in cars,
- a careful collection of significant data about the reliability of software in cars today and methodological steps to improve the reliability,
- better ways to model cars with respect to their software properties and structures during the development process,
- more sophisticated development processes incorporating recent scientific results from academia to improve the quality checking.

At the end of the workshop and also thereafter participants strongly expressed their satisfaction about the workshop and its usefulness to stimulate further research and progress in the area of automotive software engineering. Altogether the workshop was an overall success proving that the concept of the workshop accurately addressed the relevant issues and the appropriate community.

The organizers and editors extend their profound thanks to all workshop participants, authors, keynote speakers, panelists, reviewers, sponsors and members of the local organization team for their important contributions to the success of the workshop itself and of this post-proceedings volume.

March 2006   Manfred Broy
                                                              Ingolf H. Krüger
                                                           Michael Meisinger

AUTOMOTIVE SOFTWARE WORKSHOP SAN DIEGO 2004

Organizers

Manfred Broy
Ingolf H. Krüger

Referees

Scott Andrews
Luciano Baresi
Frederic Doucet
Carlo Ghezzi
Rajesh Gupta
Gabor Karsai
Luciano Lavagno
Insup Lee
Michael Meisinger
Massimiliano Menarini
Klaus D. Müller-Glaser
Edward C. Nelson
Wolfgang Pree
Insik Shin
Janos Sztipanovits

Local Arrangements

David Bareno
Martha Chavez
Diwaker Gupta
Ingolf H. Krüger
Jennifer Lee
Russell McClure
Don Peters-Coville
Sabine Rittmann
Marilyn Samms

Sponsors

California Institute for Telecommunication and Information Technology (Calit2)
National Science Foundation (NSF)
ARTIST, European Union (EU)
Deutsche Forschungsgemeinschaft (DFG)

   Deutsche
Forschungsgemeinschaft

Table of Contents

Analyzing the Worst-Case Execution Time by Abstract Interpretation of Executable Code

Christian Ferdinand[1], Reinhold Heckmann[1], and Reinhard Wilhelm[2]

[1] AbsInt Angewandte Informatik GmbH
Science Park 1, D-66123 Saarbrücken, Germany
info@absint.com
http://www.absint.com

[2] Universität des Saarlandes, Postfach 15 11 50, D-66041 Saarbrücken, Germany
wilhelm@cs.uni-sb.de
http://rw4.cs.uni-sb.de

Abstract. Determining the worst-case execution times (WCETs) of tasks in safety-critical hard real-time systems is a difficult problem. A combination of automatic analysis techniques with a few user annotations yields precise WCET estimates.

1 Introduction

Many tasks in safety-critical embedded systems have hard real-time characteristics. Failure to meet deadlines may result in the loss of life or in large damages. Utmost carefulness and state-of-the-art machinery have to be applied to make sure that all requirements are met. To do so lies in the responsibility of the system designer(s).

The problem of finding estimates (precise upper bounds) for the worst-case execution times (WCETs) of tasks in embedded applications is difficult for various reasons [1]. There is typically a large gap between the cycle times of modern microprocessors and the access times of main memory. Caches and branch target buffers are used to overcome this gap in virtually all performance-oriented processors (including high-performance microcontrollers and DSPs). Pipelines enable acceleration by overlapping the executions of different instructions. The consequence is that the execution behavior of the instructions cannot be analyzed separately since it depends on the execution history.

Cache memories usually work very well, but under some circumstances minimal changes in the program code or program input may lead to dramatic changes in cache behavior. For (hard) real-time systems, this is undesirable and possibly even hazardous. The widely used classical methods of predicting execution times are not generally applicable. Software monitoring or the dual-loop benchmark change the code, what in turn has impact on the cache behavior. Hardware simulation, emulation, or direct measurement with logic analyzers can only determine the execution time for one input. This cannot be used to infer the execution times for all possible inputs in general. Making the safe—yet for the most part—unrealistic assumption that all memory references lead to cache misses results in the execution time being overestimated by several hundred percent.

M. Broy, I.H. Krüger, and M. Meisinger (Eds.): ASWSD 2004, LNCS 4147, pp. 1–14, 2006.

Abstract interpretation can be used to efficiently compute a safe approximation for all possible cache and pipeline states that can occur at a program point. These results can be combined with ILP (Integer Linear Programming) techniques to safely predict the worst-case execution time and a corresponding worst-case execution path.

Apart from the executable program to be analyzed, the analyzers rely on user input to find a result at all, or to improve the precision of the result. The most important user annotations specify the targets of computed calls and branches and the maximum iteration counts of loops. We also present automatic analyses to determine the targets of computed branches and calls automatically in typical cases for code compiled from C and an automatic loop bound analysis for loops with constant bounds. Furthermore, we show how these analyses can be extended to handle code produced with the help of typical code generator tools widely used in the automotive area.

Sect. 2 introduces **AbsInt**'s **aiT** tool for WCET analysis. Sect. 3 describes the working of **aiT**, i.e. the various analysis algorithms. Sect. 4 presents various possibilities for user annotations that help **aiT** in doing its work. Sect. 5 deals with a side issue, namely stack analysis. Future work is discussed in Sect. 6, and Sect. 7 concludes.

2   aiT – WCET Analyzers

The **AbsInt** company has created a family of WCET analyzer tools called **aiT**. The **aiT** tools get as input an executable, user annotations as described in Sect. 4, a description of the (external) memories and buses (i.e. a list of memory areas with minimal and maximal access times), and a task (identified by a start address). A task denotes a sequentially executed piece of code (no threads, no parallelism, and no waiting for external events). This should not be confused with a task in an operating system that might include code for synchronization or communication.

The WCET analyzers compute an upper bound of the runtime of the task (assuming no interference from the outside). Effects of interrupts, IO and timer (co-)processors are not reflected in the predicted runtime and have to be considered separately (e.g., by a quantitative analysis).

In addition to the raw information about the WCET, several aspects can be visualized by the aiSee tool [2] to view detailed information delivered by the analysis.

Figure 1 shows the graphical representation of the call graph for some small example as produced by **aiT**. The calls (edges) that contribute to the worst-case runtime are marked by the color red. The computed WCET is given in CPU cycles and in microseconds provided that the cycle time of the processor has been specified.

Figure 2 shows the basic block graph of a loop. The number `max #` describes the maximal number of traversals of an edge in the worst case, while `max t` describes the maximal execution time of the basic block from which the edge originates

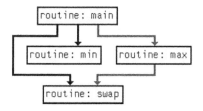

Fig. 1. Call graph with WCET results

(taking into account that the basic block is left via the edge). The worst-case path, the iteration numbers and timings are determined automatically by **aiT**.

Figure 3 shows the possible pipeline states for a basic block in this example. Such pictures are shown by **aiT** upon special demand. The large dark grey boxes correspond to the instructions of the basic block, and the smaller rectangles in them stand for individual pipeline states. Their cyclewise evolution is indicated by the strokes connecting them. Each layer in the trees corresponds to one CPU cycle. Branches in the trees are caused by conditions that could not be statically evaluated, e.g., a memory access with unknown address in presence of memory areas with different access times. On the other hand, two pipeline states fall together when details they differ in leave the pipeline. This happened for instance at the end of the second instruction, reducing the number of states from four to three.

Figure 4 shows part of the top left pipeline state from Fig. 3 in greater magnification. It displays a diagram of the architecture of the CPU (in this case a PowerPC 555) showing the occupancy of the various pipeline stages with the instructions currently being executed.

3   Worst-Case Execution Time Prediction

In this section, we describe the working of **aiT** in greater detail.

3.1   Phases of WCET Computation

In our approach [3] the determination of the WCET of a program task is composed of several phases (see Fig. 5):

- **CFG Building:** Decoding, i.e. identification of instructions, and reconstruction of the control-flow graph (CFG) from a binary program;
- **Value Analysis:** computation of address ranges for instructions accessing memory;
- **Cache Analysis:** classification of memory references as cache misses or hits [4];

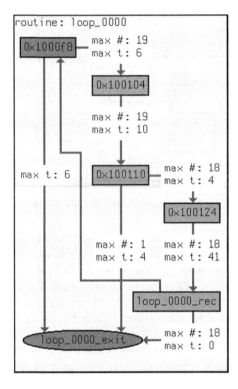

Fig. 2. Basic block graph in a loop, with timing information

- **Pipeline Analysis:** prediction of the behavior of the program on the processor pipeline [5];
- **Path Analysis:** determination of a worst-case execution path of the program [6].

The results of value analysis are used by the cache analysis to predict the behavior of the (data) cache. The results of cache analysis are used within pipeline analysis allowing the prediction of pipeline stalls due to cache misses. The combined results of the cache and pipeline analyses are used to compute the execution times of program paths. The separation of WCET determination into several phases has the additional effect that different methods tailored to the subtasks can be used. Value analysis, cache analysis, and pipeline analysis are done by abstract interpretation [7], a semantics-based method for static program analysis. Integer linear programming is used for path analysis. The various phases are presented in more detail in the following subsections.

3.2   Reconstruction of the Control Flow from Binary Programs

The Control-Flow Graph Builder (CFG Builder) has two inputs: the executable program, and a so-called AIS file containing the user annotations. In the first step a decoder reads the program, identifies the instructions and their operands,

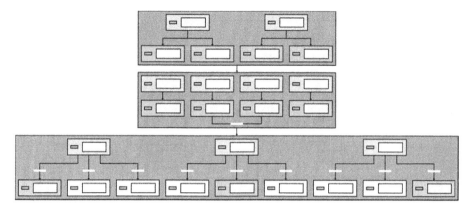

Fig. 3. Possible pipeline states in a basic block

and reconstructs the control flow [8,9]. This requires some knowledge about the underlying hardware, e.g., which instructions represent branches or calls. A subsequent *loop transformation* identifies loops and marks them for special treatment (see Sect. 3.7).

The resulting control-flow graph is annotated with the information from the AIS file needed by subsequent analyses and then translated into CRL (Control-Flow Representation Language). This annotated control-flow graph is forwarded to the various analyzers. Each analyzer adds its results to the graph by means of CRL attributes so that they are available in all subsequent analysis steps.

The decoder can find the target addresses of absolute and **pc**-relative calls and branches, but may have difficulties with target addresses computed from register contents. Thus, **aiT** uses specialized decoders that are adapted to certain code generators and/or compilers. They usually can recognize branches to a previously stored return address, and know the typical compiler-generated patterns of branches via switch tables. Yet non-trivial applications may still contain some computed calls and branches (in handwritten assembly code) that cannot be resolved by the decoder; these unresolved computed calls and branches are documented by appropriate messages and require user annotations (see Sect. 4). Such annotations may list the possible targets of computed calls and branches, or tell the decoder about the address and format of an array of function pointers or a switch table used in the computed call or branch.

3.3 Value Analysis

Value analysis tries to determine the values in the processor registers for every program point and execution context. Often it cannot determine these values exactly, but only finds safe lower and upper bounds, i.e. intervals that are guaranteed to contain the exact values. A subtask of value analysis is loop bound analysis, which tries to find the maximum iteration numbers of loops (see Sect. 3.8). The results of value analysis are also used to determine possible addresses of indirect memory accesses—an information important for cache analysis.

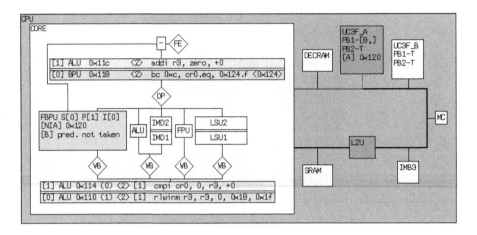

Fig. 4. Individual pipeline state

3.4   Cache Analysis

Cache analysis classifies the accesses to main memory. The analysis in our tool is based upon [4], which handles analysis of caches with LRU (Least Recently Used) replacement strategy. However, it had to be modified to reflect the non-LRU replacement strategies of common microprocessors: the pseudo-round-robin replacement policy of the ColdFire MCF 5307, and the PLRU (Pseudo-LRU) strategy of the PowerPC MPC 750 and 755. The modified algorithms distinguish between sure cache hits and unclassified accesses. The deviation from perfect LRU is the reason for the reduced predictability of the cache contents in case of ColdFire 5307 and PowerPC 750/755 compared to processors with perfect LRU caches [10].

3.5   Pipeline Analysis

Pipeline analysis models the pipeline behavior to determine execution times for a sequential flow (basic block) of instructions, as done in [5,11]. It takes into account the current pipeline state(s), in particular resource occupancies, contents of prefetch queues, grouping of instructions, and classification of memory references as cache hits or misses. The result is an execution time for each instruction in each distinguished execution context.

3.6   Path Analysis

Using the results of the micro-architecture analyses, path analysis determines a safe estimate of the WCET. The program's control flow is modeled by an integer linear program [6,12] so that the solution to the objective function is the predicted worst-case execution time for the input program. A special mapping of variable names to basic blocks in the integer linear program enables execution and traversal counts for every basic block and edge to be computed.

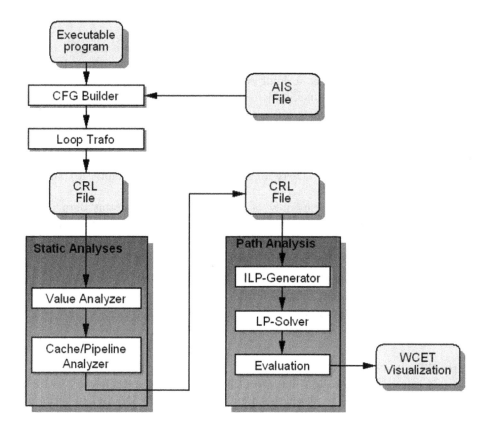

Fig. 5. Phases of WCET computation

3.7 Analysis of Loops and Recursive Procedures

Loops and recursive procedures are of special interest since programs spend most of their runtime there. Treating them naively when analyzing programs for their cache and pipeline behavior results in a high loss of precision.

Frequently the first execution of the loop body loads the cache, and subsequent executions find most of their referenced memory blocks in the cache. Because of speculative prefetching, cache contents may still change considerably during the second iteration. Therefore, the first few iterations of the loop often encounter cache contents quite different from those of later iterations. Hence it is useful to distinguish the first few iterations of loops from the others. This is done in the VIVU approach (virtual inlining, virtual unrolling) [13].

Using upper bounds on the number of loop iterations, the analyses can virtually unroll not only the first few iterations, but all iterations. The analyses can then distinguish more contexts and the precision of the results is increased—at the expense of higher analysis times.

3.8   Loop Bound Analysis

WCET analysis requires that upper bounds for the iteration numbers of all loops be known. **aiT** tries to determine the number of loop iterations by *loop bound analysis*, but succeeds in doing so for simple loops only. Bounds for the iteration numbers of the remaining loops must be provided as user annotations (see Sect. 4).

Loop bound analysis relies on a combination of value analysis (see Sect. 3.3) and pattern matching, which looks for typical loop patterns. In general, these loop patterns depend on the code generator and/or compiler used to generate the code that is being analyzed. There are special **aiT** versions adapted to various generators and compilers.

Normally, loop bounds can only be determined if all relevant data (loop counter etc.) are held in registers. The reason is that data held in memory locations might be altered by accesses to unknown memory addresses. An exception is made for code generated by known code generation tools, e.g.,

```
for((map->ctr1->low=1);(map->ctr1->low<=3);(map->ctr1->low++)){
  for((map->ctr2->low=1);(map->ctr2->low<=6);(map->ctr2->low++)){
    /* code with memory accesses via pointers ... */
  }
}
```

Here, **aiT** assumes that the generated code is well-behaved so that the memory accesses in the loop body do not affect the loop counters. To be on the safe side, **aiT** issues a message about this assumption and asks the user to verify it manually.

Another common type of loops in generated code is linear search in a sorted array, e.g.,

```
while (x > *(x_table++) ) ...
```

Here, there is the risk that x is greater than all table values so that the loop continues examining values beyond the end of the table in an uncontrolled way. Yet again, **aiT** assumes that the code generator has avoided this error situation by an extra test before the loop or by putting the largest possible value at the end of the table. Then the number of executions of the loop header is bounded by the size of the table. Again, **aiT** issues a message asking the user to verify that the assumption is valid.

4   User Annotations

Apart from the executable, **aiT** needs user input to find a result at all, or to improve the precision of the result. These user annotations may be supplied in a special file, the so-called AIS file (see Fig. 5), or as special comments in the source code (see Sect. 4.3). The most important user annotations specify the targets of computed calls and branches and the maximum iteration counts of loops (there are many other possible annotations).

4.1   Targets of Computed Calls and Branches

For a correct reconstruction of the control flow from the binary, targets of computed calls and branches must be known. **aiT** can find many of these targets automatically for code compiled from C. This is done by identifying and interpreting switch tables and static arrays of function pointers. Yet dynamic use of function pointers cannot be tracked by **aiT**, and hand-written assembly code in library functions often contains difficult computed branches. Targets for computed calls and branches that are not found by **aiT** must be specified by the user. This can be done by writing specifications of the following forms in a parameter file called AIS file:

```
INSTRUCTION ProgramPoint CALLS Target₁, ..., Targetₙ ;
INSTRUCTION ProgramPoint BRANCHES TO Target₁, ..., Targetₙ ;
```

ARM7 TDMI processors do not offer return instructions. Instead, various kinds of computed branches with the return address as target can be employed. **aiT** can recognize most of these branches as returns. The few remaining ones, mostly contained in library code, can be annotated as follows:

```
INSTRUCTION ProgramPoint IS A RETURN ;
```

Program points are not restricted to simple addresses. A program point description particularly suited for CALLS and BRANCHES specifications is   "R" + n COMPUTED   which refers to the nth computed call or branch in routine R— counted statically in the sense of increasing addresses, not dynamically following the control flow. In a similar way, targets can be specified as absolute addresses, or relative to a routine entry in the form   "R" + n BYTES   or relative to the address of the conditional branch instruction, which is denoted by PC.

Example 1. The library routine C_MEMCPY in TI's standard library for the TMS470 consists of hand-written assembly code. It contains 2 computed branches whose targets can be specified as follows:

```
instruction "C_MEMCPY" + 1 computed
branches to pc + 0x04 bytes, pc + 0x14 bytes, pc + 0x24 bytes;

instruction "C_MEMCPY" + 2 computed
branches to pc + 0x10 bytes, pc + 0x20 bytes;
```

The advantage of such relative specifications is that they work no matter what the absolute address of C_MEMCPY is.

  If the application contains an array P of function pointers, then a call P[i](x) may branch to any address contained in P. **aiT** tries to obtain the list of these addresses automatically: If the array access and the computed call in the executable are part of a small code pattern as it is typically generated by the compiler, **aiT** notices that the computed call is performed via this array. If furthermore the array contents are defined in a data segment so that they are statically available, and the array is situated in a ROM area so that its contents cannot be modified, then **aiT** automatically considers the addresses in the array as possible targets of the computed call.

If array access and computed call are too far apart or realized in an untypical way, **aiT** cannot recognize that they belong together. Similar remarks apply to computed branches via switch tables. In both cases, the array or table belonging to the computed call or branch can be declared in the AIS file. The declaration starts like the ones described above:

```
INSTRUCTION ProgramPoint CALLS VIA ArrayDescriptor ;
INSTRUCTION ProgramPoint BRANCHES VIA ArrayDescriptor ;
```

Here, the *ArrayDescriptor* describes the address and the format of the table that contains the call or branch targets. These targets are extracted from the table according to the given format rules.

4.2 Loop Bounds

WCET analysis requires that upper bounds for the iteration numbers of all loops be known. **aiT** tries to determine the number of loop iterations by *loop bound analysis*, but succeeds in doing so only for loops with constant bounds whose code matches certain patterns typically generated by the supported compilers. Bounds for the iteration numbers of the remaining loops must be provided by user annotations. A maximum iteration number of j is specified in the AIS parameter file as follows:

```
LOOP ProgramPoint  Qualifier MAX j ;
```

A *ProgramPoint* is either an address or an expression of the form `"R" + n LOOPS` which means the nth loop in routine R counted from 1. *Qualifier* is an optional information:

- **begin** indicates that the loop test is at the beginning of the loop, as for C's while-loops.
- **end** indicates that the loop test is at the end of the loop, as for C's do-while-loops.

If the qualifier is omitted, **aiT** assumes the worst case of the two possibilities, which is **begin** where the loop test is executed one more time. The **begin/end** information refers to the *executable*, not to the source code; the compiler may move the loop test from the beginning to the end, or vice versa.

Example 2.   `loop "_prime" + 1 loop end max 10 ;`
specifies that the first loop in _prime has the loop test at the end and is executed at most 10 times.

4.3 Source Code Annotations

Specifications can also be included in C source code files as special comments marked by the key string `ai:`

```
/* ai: specification₁ ; ... specificationₙ ; */
```

The names of the source files are extracted from the debug information in the executable.

Source code annotations admit a special program point or target **here**, which roughly denotes the place where the annotation occurs (due to compiler optimizations the debug information is not always precise). More exactly, **aiT** extracts the correspondence between source lines and code addresses from the executable. A **here** occurring in source line n then points to the *first* instruction associated with a line number $\geq n$.

For loop annotations, it is not required that **here** exactly denotes the loop start address. It suffices that it resolves to an address anywhere in the loop as in the following example:

```
for (i=3; i*i <= n; i += 2) {
    /* ai: loop here end max 10; */
    ... }
```

4.4   Other Annotations

Apart from branch targets and loop bounds, many other properties can be declared in parameter or source files.

- To get any WCET results at all, you must specify upper bounds for the recursion depths of all recursive routines. These specifications are similar to the loop bound specifications described above.
- Flow constraints are linear constraints for the execution counts of basic blocks. For instance,

  ```
  flow (0x100) <= 4 * (0x200);
  ```

  means that the number of executions of the block starting at address 0x100 is at most 4 times the number of executions of the block starting at 0x200. As always, relative addresses or semantic program point descriptions may be used instead of these absolute addresses.
- **aiT** can be informed about the clock rate of the microprocessor. Knowing the clock rate, **aiT** can display its results in real time units such as milliseconds. Without this information, all results are displayed in processor cycles.
- End specifications instruct **aiT** to stop reading the executable at a certain program point. A possible application is for instance to inform **aiT** that an interrupt routine called by a software interrupt does not return.
- Value analysis tries to determine register values and addresses of memory accesses. In cases it fails, information about exact addresses or address ranges may be supplied by annotations.
- You may specify that a memory area is read-only or write-only, contains data or code. You may also specify which data it contains.
- You may exclude certain routines from WCET analysis and supply their WCET directly.
- You may specify that a routine never returns (like exit).

- You may specify that a certain basic block is never executed.
- You may specify that a certain condition is always true or always false.
- Program points can be given symbolic names for later reference.

5 Stack Analysis

Apart from the timing constraints, embedded applications also face constraints on the memory usage. A possible cause of catastrophic failure is stack overflow that usually leads to run-time errors that are difficult to diagnose. The problem is that the memory area for the stack usually must be reserved by the programmer. Underestimation of the maximum stack usage leads to stack overflow, while overestimation means wasting memory resources. Measuring the maximum stack usage with a debugger is no solution since one only obtains a result for a single program run with fixed input. Even repeated measurements with various inputs cannot guarantee that the maximum stack usage is ever observed. Some, but not all compilers provide information about stack usage, but this requires the availability of the source code, and the information becomes invalid when the generated code is optimized by hand or by some automatic tool.

AbsInt's tool **StackAnalyzer** provides a solution to this problem. It uses the same decoders as **aiT** for reading the executables, and a subset of **aiT**'s annotation language. By concentrating on the value of the stack pointer during value analysis, the tool can figure out how the stack increases and decreases along the various control-flow paths. This information can be used to derive the maximum stack usage of the analyzed task. The predicted worst-case stack usages of the single tasks in a system can be used in an automated overall stack usage analysis for all tasks running on one ECU, as described in [14] for systems managed by an OSEK/VDX real-time operating system.

6 Future Work

Both WCET analysis and stack usage analysis will be extended to cover further microarchitectures. For WCET analysis, the implementation of a pipeline analysis is the major bottleneck in case of modern architectures with features such as super-scalarity, out-of-order execution, branch prediction and folding, and truly parallel execution units. At the moment, an implementation of pipeline analysis is obtained from a pipeline model by a manual coding process. To reduce the realization phase of a pipeline analysis, we are developing a framework to generate these implementations from concise specifications of the models.

The pipeline models themselves need to be specified more formally. With a formal model, analyses on the model itself are possible. With the help of such analyses, the non-determinism in the pipeline analyses can be reduced by limiting the number of successor evolutions that have to be considered for the worst case by identifying one or a few successors that may lead to the global worst case.

The predicted WCETs so far are WCETs of single tasks in one ECU. They can be used to determine an appropriate scheduling scheme for the tasks and to perform an overall schedulability analysis in order to guarantee that all timing constraints will be met (also called *timing validation*) [15]. **AbsInt** is planning to cooperate with scheduling tool providers to reach this goal in an integrated way. **aiT**'s results can be used in schedulability analysis, and in the opposite direction, information about schedules can help to make **aiT**'s results more precise w.r.t. cache and pipeline states.

7   Conclusion

aiT allows to inspect the timing behavior of (time-critical parts of) program tasks. The analysis results are determined without the need to change the code and hold for all executions (for the intrinsic cache and pipeline behavior). **aiT** takes into account the combination of all the different hardware characteristics while still obtaining tight upper bounds for the WCET of a given program in reasonable time.

aiT is a WCET tool for industrial usage. Information required for WCET estimation such as computed branch targets and loop bounds is determined by static analysis. For situations where **aiT**'s analysis methods do not succeed, a convenient specification and annotation language was developed in close cooperation with **AbsInt**'s customers. Annotations for library functions (RT, communication) and RTOS functions can be provided in separate files by the respective developers (on source level or separately).

aiT enables development of complex hard real-time systems on state-of-the-art hardware, increases safety, and saves development time. Precise timing predictions enable the most cost-efficient hardware to be chosen. As recent trends, e.g., in automotive industries (X-by-wire, time-triggered protocols) require knowledge on the WCETs of tasks, a tool like **aiT** is of high importance.

References

1. Wilhelm, R.: Determining bounds on execution times. In Zurawski, R., ed.: Handbook on Embedded Systems. CRC Press (2005) 14–1 – 14–23
2. AbsInt Angewandte Informatik GmbH: aiSee Home Page. (http://www.aisee.com)
3. Ferdinand, C., Heckmann, R., Langenbach, M., Martin, F., Schmidt, M., Theiling, H., Thesing, S., Wilhelm, R.: Reliable and precise WCET determination for a real-life processor. In: Proceedings of EMSOFT 2001, First Workshop on Embedded Software. Volume 2211 of Lecture Notes in Computer Science., Springer-Verlag (2001) 469–485
4. Ferdinand, C.: Cache Behavior Prediction for Real-Time Systems. PhD thesis, Saarland University (1997)
5. Langenbach, M., Thesing, S., Heckmann, R.: Pipeline modeling for timing analysis. In: Proceedings of the 9th International Static Analysis Symposium SAS 2002. Volume 2477 of Lecture Notes in Computer Science., Springer-Verlag (2002) 294–309
6. Theiling, H., Ferdinand, C.: Combining abstract interpretation and ILP for microarchitecture modelling and program path analysis. In: Proceedings of the 19th IEEE Real-Time Systems Symposium, Madrid, Spain (1998) 144–153

7. Cousot, P., Cousot, R.: Abstract Interpretation: A Unified Lattice Model for Static Analysis of Programs by Construction or Approximation of Fixpoints. In: Proceedings of the 4th ACM Symposium on Principles of Programming Languages, Los Angeles, California (1977)

8. Theiling, H.: Extracting safe and precise control flow from binaries. In: Proceedings of the 7th Conference on Real-Time Computing Systems and Applications, Cheju Island, South Korea (2000)

9. Theiling, H.: Generating decision trees for decoding binaries. In: Proceedings of ACM SIGPLAN LCTES/OM 2001, ACM Press (2001) 112–120

10. Heckmann, R., Langenbach, M., Thesing, S., Wilhelm, R.: The influence of processor architecture on the design and the results of WCET tools. Proceedings of the IEEE **91** (2003) 1038–1054 Special Issue on Real-Time Systems.

11. Schneider, J., Ferdinand, C.: Pipeline behavior prediction for superscalar processors by abstract interpretation. In: Proceedings of ACM SIGPLAN LCTES'99. (1999) 35–44

12. Theiling, H.: ILP-based interprocedural path analysis. In Sangiovanni-Vincentelli, A.L., Sifakis, J., eds.: Proceedings of EMSOFT 2002, Second International Conference on Embedded Software. Volume 2491 of Lecture Notes in Computer Science., Springer-Verlag (2002) 349–363

13. Martin, F., Alt, M., Wilhelm, R., Ferdinand, C.: Analysis of Loops. In Koskimies, K., ed.: Proceedings of the International Conference on Compiler Construction (CC'98). Volume 1383 of Lecture Notes in Computer Science., Springer-Verlag (1998) 80–94

14. Janz, W.: Das OSEK Echtzeitbetriebssystem, Stackverwaltung und statische Stackbedarfsanalyse. In: Embedded World, Nuremberg, Germany (2003)

15. Stankovic, J.A.: Real-Time and Embedded Systems. ACM 50th Anniversary Report on Real-Time Computing Research. (1996) http://www-ccs.cs.umass.edu/sdcr/rt.ps.

Quality Assurance and Certification of Software Modules in Safety Critical Automotive Electronic Control Units Using a CASE-Tool Integration Platform

Klaus D. Mueller-Glaser[1], Clemens Reichmann[1], Markus Kuehl[2], and Stefan Benz[3]

[1] Institut für Technik der Informationsverarbeitung (ITIV)
Universität Karlsruhe, Engesserstrasse 5, D-76128 Karlsruhe, Germany
{Mueller-Glaser, Reichmann}@itiv.uni-karlsruhe.de
[2] Forschungszentrum Informatik (FZI),
Haid-und-Neustrasse 10-14, D-76128 Karlsruhe, Germany
kuehl@fzi.de
[3] Robert Bosch GmbH, P.O. Box 10 60 50, D-70049 Stuttgart, Germany
Stefan.Benz@de.bosch.com

Abstract. Up to 70 electronic control units (ECU's) serve for safety and comfort functions in a car. Communicating over different bus systems most ECU's perform close loop control functions and reactive functions and have to fulfill hard real time constraints. Some ECU's controlling on board entertainment/office systems are software intensive, incorporating millions of lines of code. The challenge for the design of those distributed and networked control units is to define all requirements and constraints, understand and analyze those manifold interactions between the control units, the car and the environment (driver, road, weather) in normal as well as stress situations (crash). To improve the design of safety critical ECU's we propose an enhanced development process (double-V-model). The use of different modeling descriptions for closed loop control, reactive systems and software intensive systems requires a CASE-tool integration platform. We have developed "GeneralStore" as a platform to support model driven design with hetero-geneous models in a design process which is concurrent and distributed between the automotive manufacturer and several suppliers.

1 Introduction

More than 70 electronic control units (ECU's) serve for safety and comfort functions in a luxury car. Communicating over different bus systems (e.g. CAN class C and B [8] , LIN [25], MOST [27], Bluetooth [3], [6]). Many ECU's are dealing with close loop control functions as well as reactive functions, they are interfacing to sensors and actuators and have to fulfill safety critical hard real time constraints (thus the software is running under a real time operating and network management system like OSEK/VDX [31] on a standard hardware platform). Other ECU's controlling the onboard infotainment system (video- and audio-entertainment, office-in-the-car with according internet and voice communication, navigation) are really software intensive, incorporating millions of lines of code. All ECU's are connected to the

M. Broy, I.H. Krüger, and M. Meisinger (Eds.): ASWSD 2004, LNCS 4147, pp. 15–30, 2006.

different buses which in turn are connected through a central gateway to enable the communication among all ECU's.

As new functions in future cars require communication to traffic guidance systems, road condition information systems as well as car to car communication, the software intensive infotainment ECU's will be directly coupled to power train and body control ECU's, even forming closed loop control. Thus, the design of these future systems need to combine methodologies and computer aided design tools for reactive systems and closed loop control systems as well as software intensive systems.

The challenge for the design of those distributed and networked control units is to find and define all requirements and constraints, to understand and analyze those manifold interactions between the many control units, the car and the environment (road, weather etc.) in normal as well as in stress situations (crash), to perform failure mode and effects analysis and to ensure fail safe and fail operational units for safety critical functions. The development process, which is concurrent and distributed between the automotive manufacturer and several suppliers, requires a well understood life-cycle model and a strictly controlled design methodology and using computer aided engineering and design tools to its largest extent.

Design methodologies used today in the automotive industry are focused on the design of distributed functions. Currently, safety and reliability issues are not taken into account from the very beginning of the development process. In the automotive industry the V-model [40] is a well recognized and widely used life cycle model. To include safety and reliability issues from the very beginning we propose in chapter 2 to extend the V-model into a double-V-model where the existing first V describes the development of functions complemented by and interrelated to the second V which handles safety and reliability issues. A well defined information exchange between the activities and products of the two Vs take care of the system safety assessment process, fault tree analysis and failure mode and effects analysis. The methodology is based on certification considerations of complex aircraft systems (SAE ARP 4754 standard [18] and IEC 61508 standard [17]) tailored for automotive applications.

Handling safety issues earlier in the design cycle is just one of the major challenges in automotive electronics. Due to the different description methods preferred for the development of closed loop control functions (power train control), reactive functions (body functions) and software intensive functions (car-infotainment) support is needed to handle heterogeneous models in a model based design methodology. For that purpose we have developed the CASE tool integration platform "GeneralStore". As described in chapter 3 GeneralStore is a MOF, XMI based repository to couple heterogeneous models developed with tools like Matlab/Simulink/Stateflow, Statemate, UML based tools and generic XMI tools. GeneralStore uses commercial code generators as well as a proprietary code generator for handling structural and behavioral descriptions in UML. GeneralStore is developed using Java and the MySQL or Oracle database system. GeneralStore offers functions for check-in/check-out, automatic wrapping, code generation, compile and link as well as versioning and configuration of software modules. Using the double-V development model and GeneralStore we will enhance the development process for safety critical applications and provide more efficiency in model based design.

2   A Design Methodology for Safety Relevant ECU's

The standard process for the development of automotive electronic systems is based on the "V Model '97", a life cycle process model that is the development standard for embedded electronic systems of the Federal Republic of Germany [40]. Originally intended for information and communication systems it was adapted for other domains, including the automotive domain. However the sequences of design and verification steps is neither standardized nor formalized throughout the automotive domain. Almost every OEM and supplier uses a slightly different design method. In the automotive industry currently large efforts are made to enhance the development of safety critical electronic systems. The aerospace industry (a domain with very standardized and formal development processes) has a lot more experience with safety-critical systems. Aerospace development processes have both function and safety of an aerospace system as the center of focus [24] (Fig.1).

However, the aerospace processes cannot be used directly in the automotive domain, as the boundary conditions and the requirements for safety and reliability in these two domains are different. For example hazard analysis for an airplane explicitly distinguishes between different flight phases (start, cruise, landing). The according phases for cars (start, accelerate, cruise, braking) generally don't make sense. For cars different driving situations are more relevant e.g. for a steer-by-wire system: driving straight ahead, driving curve, pass maneuver, reversing etc., in principle distinguish whether or not the steering wheel needs to be turned or not. Also road conditions should be considered (rain, aquaplaning, ice, off road, gravel, sand, road hole, flange groove).

Besides different analysis processes the most important differentiation is the very low production volume of electronic control units in an airplane in comparison to automotive electronic systems (several thousands vs. several millions), therefore, cost for more hardware components in an airplane preponderate much less than labor-intensive and protracted development and test of a new concept. Safety and reliability requirements in airplanes allow for expensive redundancy concepts. Redundancy is necessary in both domains, however, the triple-triple modular hardware redundancy for the primary flight control in a large passenger plane, e.g. the Boeing 777, is by far too expensive in automotive applications, so, double hardware redundancy is common in cars.

A basic property of system development in aerospace domain is the certification of both, the design process and the designed system (usually by a third party like the Federal Aviation Association FAA). We propose a similar approach to an adapted methodology for the automotive domain which considers safety equally with function and can be described as "double V model". It is based on the V-model [40] (Fig.2 shows the V-model with focus on software development), however, a second V with elements that have a special focus on safety and reliability is added to the original V and connected to it at several appropriate places in the development process. The concepts underlying the additional elements were taken from the aerospace domain and adapted to automotive conditions. Figure 3 gives an overview on the proposed design methodology.

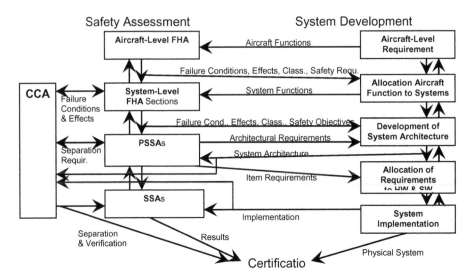

Fig. 1. SAE ARP 4754 standard: safety assessment in parallel to system development

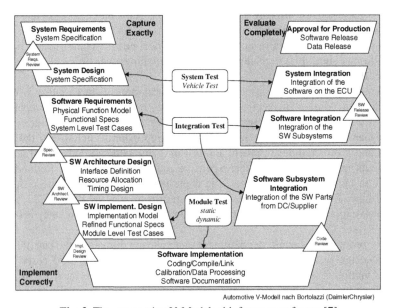

Fig. 2. The automotive V-Model with focus on software [7]

In the functional hazard assessment the functional safety requirements for the system are assessed. For this purpose the potential hazards of system functions are determined and classified and, if possible, reliability requirements are derived. Non functional safety requirements (e.g. costs, maintainability, use of standard platforms, mechanical properties like weight and shape) are not considered in the functional

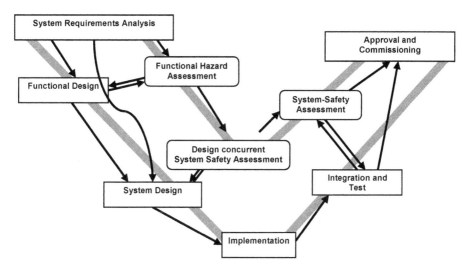

Fig. 3. Overview proposed design methodology

hazard assessment. By a systematic procedure in the early steps of the system development process continuity to subsequent process steps is assured. Based on the system requirements analysis during the functional hazard assessment the system is categorized into risk classes. For this purpose the system is brought in context with its environment, then impacts on the environment and of the environment on the system are analyzed. Like in the concurrent process step functional design the assessment here focuses on the system's functions only. Based on the function list that was generated in the functional design, the corresponding failure conditions are identified and described. For every function there may be several possible failure conditions depending on the system's environmental conditions. The effects of these failure conditions result in possible risks and hazards. These hazards are classified into risk classes based on their severity. This classification is a very critical point in the functional hazard assessment. It should be carried out using a methodology that is adapted to the boundary conditions of the automotive industry (e.g. "CARTRONIC safety analysis" (CSA) according to [5]). Usually a risk graph or decision tree is used; the risk graph of CSA with 5 safety levels ("SL") is shown in figure 4.

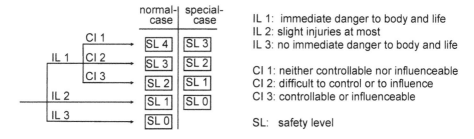

Fig. 4. Risk Graph used in CARTRONIC Safety Analysis

The design concurrent system safety assessment is a systematic examination of the system architectures that were proposed during conceptual system design. The goal is a thorough examination whether or not the architecture fulfills the quantitative and qualitative requirements of the functional hazard assessment or if faults or failures can possibly lead to system hazards. The basic idea of the quantitative assessment is the replacement of safety requirements by corresponding reliability requirements in the functional hazard assessment, for example the safety levels SL 1, 2, 3, 4 demand for failure rates less than 10^{-6}/h, 10^{-7}/h, 10^{-8}/h and 10^{-9}/h, respectively [17].

If no quantitative assessment is possible the examination has to take place qualitatively and quantitative results have to be estimated. It is evaluated whether the system architecture and the planned concept design can reasonably be expected to meet the safety requirements and objectives. The methods used are Fault Tree Analysis (FTA) and Markov Analysis (MA) for reliability issues and Failure Mode and Effects Analysis (FMEA) for safety conditions. Common cause errors are examined by common cause analysis (CCA). In addition also other potential hazards than functional hazards are examined. So it is determined whether the system concept design contains additional hazards, esp. hazards that are generated by the system design itself. The method used for this purpose is FMEA. Based on the results of these analyses safety requirements for the design on lower levels (also for hardware and software) and for other systems involved are derived. That way it is ensured that the implementation of the systems fully fulfills its requirements for safety and reliability. Then the design concurrent system safety assessment is repeated for lower system levels. This procedure is supported by several data sources. The most famous database is the MIL-Handbook 217 [9]; though officially discontinued for several years it is still used widely in the civil and military aviation industry. Other databases include the MIL Handbook 978 "NASA Parts Application Handbook", RAC "Non Electronic Parts Reliability Data", RAC "Failure Mode/Mechanism Distribution" and Rome Laboratory's "Reliability Engineer's Toolkit" which provide failure rates for many component types. A major database used in the automotive domain is the "Reliability Data Handbook" of the "Union Technique de l'Electricite" (UTE) [38]. It is to be expected that it will be the successor of the MIL Handbook 217. An example for the application of the UTE handbook can be seen in [38]. In parallel to the process step integration-and-test in system safety assessment the system's conformance to its safety requirements is checked. This is accomplished by the verification of the system's design requirements established in the functional hazard assessment, by a review of the hazard classification of the functional hazard assessment and by verification and validation of other safety requirements. The process of verification and validation as it is known from the V-model takes place in three steps. Here the functional part as well as the non-functional but non-safety part is assessed during integration and test, the issues concerning safety are tested here in the system safety assessment. Generally speaking the procedure in the system safety assessment is very similar to the one during the design concurrent system safety assessment. The same tools are used, but the main difference is now that the system in focus is a physically implemented, real and running system. The same fault tree as in the design concurrent system safety assessment is used again, but the failure rates of the elements in the fault tree no longer come from a database but from the experiences with the real system components. As with system design and design concurrent system safety assessment the process switches iteratively back and forth between integration and test and system safety assessment. The system is integrated and tested on its correct function, parallel the system's safety properties are proven. For this purpose the system's parts have to fulfill the requirements of the system requirements analysis and especially the quantitative reliability requirements of the functional hazard assessment. The review is done by a systematic examination of the system, its architecture and its realization by various methods of verification and validation (for example testing, fault injection or formal methods). So it is possible to prove that the system fulfills its safety requirements.

As an example for functional hazard assessment two functions of a steer-by-wire system are shown. In turning the steering wheel the driver requests a certain direction in setting an according steering angle. The effective steering moment at the wheels is fed back to the driver by an according steering wheel moment as a haptic feedback. Thus, there are two functions in the function list: 1. steering and 2. feedback steering wheel moment. Analysis identifies the following hazards for function 1: 1.A vehicle does not steer, 1.B steering mechanism blocked, 1.C vehicle steering angle is different from steering wheel set point, and for function 2: 2.A no feedback of steering wheel moment, 2.B steering wheel rotates by itself, 2.C steering wheel blocked. Analysis of

Table 1. Hazard analysis for function steering

No.	Function	Hazard	Constraint	Effects	SL
1.A.1	steering	Vehicle does not steer	Steering function currently in use	Death or severe injury of one or more persons possible. Situation is not controllable. Normal case incidence.	4
1.A.2			Steering function currently not in use	Death or severe injury of one or more persons possible. Situation is not controllable. Special case incidence.	3
1.B.1		Steering mechanism blocked	Steering function currently in use	Death or severe injury of one or more persons possible. Situation is not controllable. Normal case incidence.	4
1.B.2			Steering function currently not in use	Death or severe injury of one or more persons possible. Situation is not controllable. Special case incidence.	3
1.C.1		Vehicle steering angle different from steering wheel set point	Steering function Currently in use	Death or severe injury of one or more persons possible. Situation is not controllable. Normal case incidence.	4
1.C.2			Steering function currently not in use	Death or severe injury of one or more persons possible. Situation is difficult to control. Normal case incidence.	3

safety levels results in SL4 for function 1 and SL3 for function 2, as a quantitative reliability requirement the maximum failure rate for steering is 10^{-9}/h and 10^{-8}/h respectively. Table 1 shows a further refinement of this analysis.

So far we presented the conceptual scheme for a methodology for function-safety-codesign of automotive ECU's. Handling safety issues earlier in the design cycle is just one of the major challenges in automotive electronics. Due to the different description methods actually used in ECU design, support is needed to handle heterogeneous models in a model based design methodology. For that purpose we have developed the CASE tool integration platform "GeneralStore" which will be described in chapter 3.

3   GeneralStore - A CASE Tool Integration Platform

The integration platform GeneralStore is a tool that assists a seamless development process starting with a model and ending with executable code. The software features coupling of subsystems on model level from the above mentioned modeling domains. In addition to object-oriented modeling for software intensive components in embedded systems it supports time-discrete and time-continuous modeling concepts. Our approach provides structural and behavioral modeling with front-end tools and simulation/emulation utilizing back-end tools. Using commercial and proprietary automatic code generators prototype software can be brought into operation on standard hardware platforms rapidly. The Unified Modeling Language (UML) metamodel is used for storing CASE data in a Meta Object Facility (MOF) object repository whereas XMI (XML Metadata Interchange format) is used to interchange this data with UML-CASE-tools. The CASE-tool chain we present in this paper further supports concurrent engineering including versioning and configuration management. It provides adaptors for the tools MATLAB/Simulink/Stateflow and ARTiSAN Real-Time Studio [2], as well as an importer/exporter of UML/XMI. Utilizing the UML notation for an overall system design cycle, the focus of this paper lies on the coupling of heterogeneous subsystems and on a new code generation and coupling approach. While several repository based model-management approaches exist ([1][32][34]) and model driven design is subject to related work ([10][20][21][22][23]) to our knowledge GeneralStore is the only existing platform allowing heterogeneous concurrent engineering with executable models.

3.1   Metamodeling

In our approach the whole system is described as an instance of one particular meta-model in one notation. The related metamodel has to cover all three domains: time-discrete, time-continuous, and software. The Unified Modeling Language is an Object Management Group (OMG) standard [29] which is a widely applied industry standard to model object-oriented software. Abstract syntax, well-formed rules, the Object Constraint Language (OCL) and informal semantic descriptions specify UML. As we will point out later, we use this notation to store the overall model while ECU-designers still use domain adequate modeling languages (e.g. signal flow diagram, state charts, UML, etc.), which fit best her/his design problem.

The UML specification provides XML Metadata Interchange format (XMI) [30] to enable easy interchange of metadata between modeling tools and metadata repositories in distributed heterogeneous environments. XMI integrates three key industry standards: the eXtensible Markup Language (XML), a W3C standard [41], the UML, and the Meta Object Facility (MOF) [28], an OMG standard which is used to specify metamodels.

One key aspect of UML is the four layered metamodeling architecture (Fig. 5) for general-purpose manipulation of data and metadata in distributed object repositories. This makes it suitable for a universal object-oriented modeling approach. Each layer is an abstraction of the underlying layer with the top layer (M3) at the highest abstraction level. The bottom layer (M0) comprises the information that we wish to describe, e.g., the embedded system, the data, or the execution code of a program. In our field this is typically the source code in different languages, e.g., JAVA or C++, which executes on the target machine. On the model layer (M1) there is the meta-data of the M0 layer, the so-called model. Object-oriented software is typically described on the M1 layer as an UML model. The meta-model on the M2 layer consists of descriptions that define the structure and semantics of meta-data (e.g., the UML model). These are the metamodels, e.g., UML 1.4 or UML 1.5, and define the language respectively notation for describing different kinds of data (M1). Finally, at the M3 layer there is the meta-meta-model MOF. It is used to describe meta-models and define their structure, syntax, and semantic. It is an object-oriented language for defining meta-data. MOF is self-describing. In other words, MOF uses its own metamodeling constructs.

3.2 Integration Platform

Fig. 6 and Fig. 7 show the integration platform GeneralStore. The setup of GeneralStore follows a 3-tier architecture. On the lowest layer (database layer) the commercial object-relational database management system ORACLE respectively MySQL was selected. On the business layer we provide user authentication, transaction management, object versioning, and configuration management. GeneralStore uses MOF as its database schema for storing UML artifacts. Inside the database layer an abstraction interface keeps GeneralStore independent from the given database.

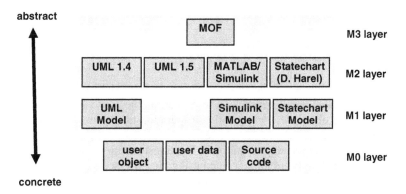

Fig. 5. Four-layer metamodeling architecture

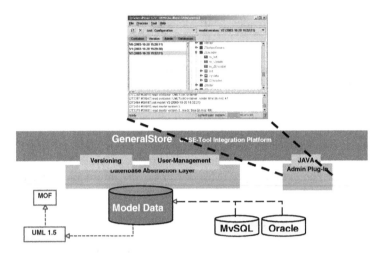

Fig. 6. CASE tool integration platform GeneralStore: model database handling view

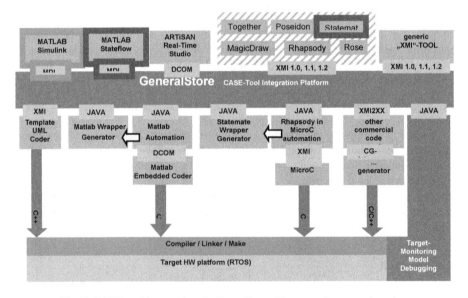

Fig. 7. CASE tool integration platform GeneralStore: code generation view

While interim objects on the business layer enclose MOF elements, the CASE adaptor stays thin and highly reusable. These interim objects are used to enable object identity to handle object versioning and configuration management. On the business layer of *GeneralStore* the mediator pattern [12] is used to keep the CASE-tool integration simple and its adaptor uniform. The transformations for specific notations supported by CASE-tools are implemented using plug-ins (see top of Fig. 7).

On the presentation layer *GeneralStore* provides three principal CASE-tool adapters:

1. MATLAB/Simulink/Stateflow [37] was selected for the control system design domain and the integration is done using the proprietary model file (MDL).

2. Generic and specialized XMI importer/exporter filters of *.xmi11 files: Here we use XSLT transformations [35] to adopt the tool specific interpretation of the UML and XMI standard. The UML CASE-tools we have chosen are Together (Borland), Poseidon (Gentleware), MagicDraw (No Magic, Inc.), Rhapsody in C++/JAVA (iLogix), and Rational Rose (IBM). Statemate (i-Logix) [19] was chosen in the time-discrete domain.

3. COM based integration of ARTiSAN Real-Time Studio [2]: This UML CASE-tool was selected because of its focus on embedded real time systems.

All tools, except Statemate, which allows only export of XMI files, are linked to the *GeneralStore* architecture in a bidirectional way.

The code generation plug-ins (Template Coder, Embedded Coder, and Rhapsody in MicroC) controls the transformation into source code (Fig.7). Their wrapper generators are automatically building the interface to the UML model.

For model management and CASE-tool control, *GeneralStore* offers a system hierarchy browser. Since the internal data model representation of *GeneralStore* is UML, *GeneralStore* offers a system browser for all UML artifacts of the current design. Due to the large amount of MOF objects (e.g., a PT1 subsystem transformed out of Matlab/Simulink with all internal parameters needs about 10,000 XMI entities), *GeneralStore* offers design domain specific hierarchy browsers, e.g., a system/subsystem hierarchy view for structural or time-continuous design, or a package hierarchy view for software design.

3.3 Code Generation and Coupling

There are highly efficient commercial code generators on the market. In safety critical systems certificated code generators have to be used to fulfill the requirements. The *GeneralStore* platform allows partitioning of the whole system into subsystems. Thus we enable the usage of different domain specific code generators. Each code generator has benefits in specialized application fields.

We follow the Model Driven Architecture (MDA) approach: Transforming a Platform Independent Model (PIM) to the Platform Specific Model (PSM).

For control-systems there are commercial code generators like Target Link (from dSPACE GmbH [11]), Embedded Coder (from Mathworks, Inc. [37]) or ECCO (from ETAS GmbH [14]). In the time-discrete domain we utilize the code generator of Statemate (Rhapsody in MicroC from I-Logix). In the software domain commercial code generators only generate the stubs of the static UML model while behavioral functionality has to be implemented by the software engineer. As we focus on a completely generated executable specification, it is necessary to generate code out of the overall model. Therefore we provide a code generator as a *GeneralStore* plug-in to enable structural and behavioral code generation directly from a UML model. The body specification is done formally in the Method Definition Language (MeDeLa), which is a high level action language based on Java syntax. It suits the action semantics defined by the OMG since UML version 1.5 as the concrete syntax.

Currently *GeneralStore* supports Embedded Coder for closed-loop models, Rhapsody in MicroC for state charts, and a template coder for the UML domain (see

Fig. 7). Our template code generator is using the Velocity engine to generate Java or C++ source code. Velocity is an Apache open source project focused on HTML code generation [39]. It provides macros, loops, conditions, and callbacks to the data model's business layer. One of its strengths is the speed when rendering.

Using the templates, the structure of the UML model is rendered to code. The behavioral specification is done with MeDeLa. It is transformed to the according Abstract Syntax Tree (AST). Then the AST is traversed as the Velocity template renders each statement or expression. It is possible to access the whole UML model from the template. Up to now, we use class diagrams and state diagrams.

Different domains have interactions, e.g., signal inspection, adoption of control system parameters at runtime, or sending messages between time-discrete and software artifacts. Those interfaces are defined in the different models and the coupling definitions are done in the UML model. The developer of such a subsystem is able to explicitly define which events, signals, data, and parameters can be accessed from the outside (the UML model). After the definition in the specific domain (e.g., closed-loop control system design) is done the notation is automatically transformed to the UML. For the discrete subsystem domain this works analogously.

The wrapper generator collects all the information about the interface in this model and generates artifacts, which represent the interface in UML. This includes the behavioral part of the access, which is done with MeDeLa. The developer uses the UML template mechanism to specify the general access mechanism for a specific type of interface. This is highly customizable. Thus the code generation provides a highly flexible mechanism for modeling domain interfaces.

3.4 IP Software Module Certification

Automotive ECU-software development is mainly done by ECU suppliers, whereas original equipment manufacturers (OEM's) usually develop requirements and later on do the integration and test. More and more libraries of functions are built up implementing software modules portable to several standard hardware platforms. However, these function libraries must be quality assured. To assist future IP-software module exchange between OEM and tier 1 and tier 2 suppliers based on the new industry standard AutoSAR – Automotive Open System Architecture [42], we are currently working on the development of a software-module certification procedure incorporating tools for rule checking (e.g. for programming guidelines as MISRA-C), static and dynamic software tests as well as incorporating model checking and abstract interpretation in a seamless way into the software development flow. Use of automatic code generators simplifies the certification process, however, the desirable certification of automatic code generators themselves is in a early stage.

Model based ECU-software development is still not standard. Also, a lot of legacy code exists. As writing static and dynamic software-unit-tests or module-tests may take even more time than implementing the function itself, and as test coverage is critical for safety related functions we are interested in incorporating new test methods. Abstract interpretation is such a method which, as commercial tools now are available, should be used already in early development phases to help discover runtime errors without the need to manually writing test cases. We have integrated the abstract interpretation tool Polyspace C-Verifier [33] within three established

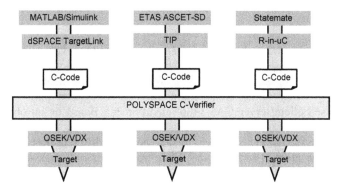

Fig. 8. Abstract interpretation verifier within established automotive tool chains

automotive tool chains (Fig. 8) [14][19][37] in such a way that a seamless automatic design and verification process flow is possible. First results on abstract interpretation of new software modules proved the value. Even when testing ECU legacy code a remarkable number of runtime faults has been detected.

3.5 Experimental Results

GeneralStore is currently in beta-site evaluation in the automotive industry. Results so far are very promising, however, thorough investigations on performance limits and other limits are still under investigation. Also we started investigating other applications domains like industrial automation systems and biomedical engineering systems.

As an example, we were quite surprised about the large amount of MOF objects generated, e.g. an empty model transformed out of Matlab/Simulink already generates 3783 XMI entities because of the many tool internal parameters normally not visible to the user. A simple integrator block needs 405 entities, a basic PID-block can count up to 2786 entities. However, describing many instantiated blocks of the same kind, the XMI entities increase is linear and scales well even to very large designs. The description of an autosampler (robot arm) with closed loop and reactive functions for a biochemical analysis system, for example, showed a total of 44239 XMI entities. The description of a passenger car for hardware-in-the-loop tests in Matlab/Simulink (>8 Megabyte .mdl file) generated more than 4 million entities. However, today's powerful database systems still perform very well with that amount of data items. Thus, GeneralStore currently is the basis for the development of a new domain specific design tool for distributed ECU's in passenger cars. The "E/E-Concept Tool" [4] allows to explore the design space for electrical/electronic systems during the concept phase of system design. It covers five different levels of abstraction, the "feature list level" (tangible customer benefits), the "feature-function-network level", the "function network level", the "component level" and the "wiring harness level".

4 Conclusion

The CASE-Tool integration platform *GeneralStore* combined with a universal object-oriented modeling approach supports the concurrent development of embedded electronic systems in all design phases. We showed how heterogeneous system descriptions in different notations could work as integrated parts of an object repository based client/server CASE-tool environment. Based on an object diagram representation, time-continuous subsystems and software components can be modeled using one single metamodel. A direct linkage between different description domains is possible on an abstract model level. While transforming all subsystem parts to an uniform object notation, adding additional model information to time-continuous blocks will enable system designers to start with system simulation early in the design process.

Embedded electronic systems can be subdivided in time-discrete, time-continuous, and software domains. Each domain uses its specific notation. A highly flexible design process was described to integrate those notations, which are supported by different CASE-tools. The glue between the domains is modeled in UML. Finally the overall system is transformed to source code with the assistance of commercial code generators in addition to our own UML template based code generator.

An often-needed feature and simultaneously a drawback of project file-based CASE-tools (e.g., Rhapsody, Simulink/Stateflow) is the lack of CASE-tool assisted concurrent engineering. Using the presented CASE-tool backend *GeneralStore* together with MATLAB/Simulink, an interim project file is created each time a designer checks out a part of the model. This is possible at any specific model hierarchy point. The checked out subsystem hierarchy becomes protected. Other designers still have read access to the last version of this subsystem and can obtain read/write access to other subsystems in the project hierarchy.

One major drawback of using UML/MOF from XMI as a metamodel for system description is the deficiency of a standardized graphical representation for class and object diagrams. Up to now, this is one of the most requested topics for UML 2.0 and the next XMI generation. On the other side, using XMI and the UML metamodel for the description of embedded systems enables model exchange with other CASE-tools. Today, at least 10 software CASE-tools are on the market, which can handle XMI descriptions from the information point of view (import of a model without graphical description).

Future work has to focus on the definition of a tailored design process and the integration of CASE-tools for requirements management (e.g., DOORS from Quality System and Software Inc.) and especially integrating seamlessly the proposed double-V-model for safety-relevant ECU's.

References

[1] Agrawal, A., Karsai, G., Ledeczi, A.: *An End-to-End Domain-Driven Software Development Framework*, 18th Annual ACM SIGPLAN Conference on Object-Oriented Programming, Systems, Languages, and Applications (OOPSLA), Domain-Driven Development Track, Anaheim, CA, October, 2003.

[2]   Artisan homepage: http://www.artisansw.com

[3]   Automotive buses: http://www.interfacebus.com/Design_Connector_Automotive.html

[4]   Belschner, R., Freess, J., Mroßko, M.: *Ganzheitlicher Entwicklungsansatz für Entwurf, Dokumentation und Bewertung von E/E-Architekturen*. In Tagungsband des 12. Internationalen Kongresses Elektronik im Kraftfahrzeug, VDI Berichte, 1907, 225-235, Düsseldorf, 2005.

[5]   Bertram T., Dominke P., Müller B.: *The Safety-Related Aspect of Cartronic*. SAE World Congress, Session Code PC26, 1999

[6]   Bluetooth homepage: http://www.bluetooth.com

[7]   Bortolazzi, J.: *Systems Engineering for Automotive Electronics*. Lecture Notes, Dep. of EEIT, University of Karlsruhe, Germany, 2003

[8]   CAN homepage: http://www.can.bosch.com

[9]   Department of Defense. *MIL-Handbook 21: Reliability Prediction of Electronic Equipment*. 1995

[10] Dörr, H.; Schürr, A.; Altheide, F.: *Requirements to a Framework for sustainable Integration of System*, EuSEC, Toulouse, 2002.

[11] dSPACE Inc. homepage: http://www.dspaceinc.com/ww/en/inc/home.htm

[12] E. Gamma et al.: *Design Patterns - elements of reusable object-oriented software*; Addison-Wesley, 1994

[13] Edler, F., Frese, Th.: *Systematic Safety Design Process for Distributed Vehicle Systems*. In Tagungsband des 12. Internationalen Kongresses Elektronik im Kraftfahrzeug, VDI Berichte, 1907, 225-235, Düsseldorf, 2005.

[14] ETAS homepage: http://en.etasgroup.com

[15] Hauser, J.: *Development of Highly complex Control Systems at BMW Group*, Competence Exchange Symposium 2004, Juni 2004.

[16] Hörner, H., Raisch, A., Meili, O.: *Basic Software Components in AUTOSAR – a Solid Foundation*. In Tagungsband des 12. Internationalen Kongresses Elektronik im Kraftfahrzeug, VDI Berichte, 1907, 225-235, Düsseldorf, 2005.

[17] http://www.iee.org/oncomms/pn/functionalsafety/HLD.pdf

[18] http://www.sae.org/servlets/productDetail?PROD_TYP=STD&PROD_CD=ARP4754

[19] I-Logix homepage: http://www.ilogix.com

[20] Kalnins, A., Barzdins, J., et al.: *Business Modeling Language GRAPES-BM and Related CASE Tools*. Proceedings of Baltic DB&IS'96, Institute of Cybernetics, Tallinn, 1996.

[21] Karsai, G., Agrawal, A., Shi, F., Sprinkle, J.: *On the Use of Graph Transformations for the Formal Specification of Model Interpreters*, Journal of Universal Computer Science, Special issue on Formal Specification of CBS, 2003.

[22] Karsai, G.: *A Challenge and Opportunity for Model-based Software Development*, Institute for Software Integrated Systems, Vanderbilt University, Automotive Software Workshop, San Diego, 2004

[23] Kleppe, A.; Warmer, J.; Blast, W.: *MDA Explained - The Model Driven Architecture: Practice and Promise*; Addison-Wesley; ISBN 0-321-19442-X, 2003

[24] Knepper, R.: *The Safety and Reliability Process in the Civil Aircraft Industry*. TechnicalReport, DaimlerChrysler Aerospace Airbus GmbH, Hamburg.

[25] LIN homepage: http://www.lin-subbus.org

[26] Moser, W.: *Motronic-Software / the key to a high performing engine management*, ETAS Symposium 2004, BOSCH Gasoline Systems, 2004.

[27] MOST homepage: http://www.mostcooperation.com

[28] Object Management Group: *OMG / Meta Object Facility (MOF)* V1.4, 2001

[29] Object Management Group: *OMG / Unified Modeling Language (UML)* V1.4, 2001

[30] Object Management Group: *OMG / XML Metadata Inter-change (XMI)* V1.0, 2000

[31] OSEK/VDX homepage: http://www.osek-vdx.org

[32] Petrov, I., Jablonski, S.: *An OMG MOF based Repository System with Querying Capability - the iRM Project.* iiWAS 2004, Jakarata, Indoesien, 27-29 September 2004

[33] Polyspace homepage   http://www.polyspace.com

[34] Porres, I.: *A Toolkit for Manipulating UML Models. Software and Systems Modeling*, Springer Verlag, 2(4):262-277, Dec. 2003

[35] Sussman, D., Kay, M.: *XSLT Programmer's Reference*, WROX, 2001.

[36] Telelogic Inc. homepage: http://www.telelogic.com/

[37] The Mathworks homepage: http://mathworks.com

[38] Union Technique de L'Electricite: *RDF2000: Reliability Data Handbook 2000*

[39] Velocity template engine: http://jakarta.apache.org/velocity/

[40] V-Model homepage: http://www.v-modell.iabg.de/vm97.htm#ENGL

[41] World Wide Web Consortium (W3C) homepage: http://www.w3.com/Consortium

[42] World Wide Web homepage AUTOSAR http://www.autosar.org

On the Fault Hypothesis for a Safety-Critical Real-Time System

H. Kopetz

Institut für Technische Informatik, TU Wien
A 1040 Wien, Treitlstrasse 3
hk@vmars.tuwien.ac.at

Abstract. A safety-critical real-time computer system must provide its services with a dependability that is much better than the dependability of any one of its constituent components. This challenging goal can only be achieved by the provision of fault tolerance. The design of any fault-tolerant system proceeds in four distinct phases. In the first phase the fault hypothesis is shaped, i.e. assumptions are made about the types and numbers of faults that must be tolerated by the planned system. In the second phase an architecture is designed that tolerates the specified faults. In the third phase the architecture is implemented and the functions and fault-tolerance mechanisms are validated. Finally, in the fourth phase it has to be confirmed experimentally that the assumptions contained in the fault-hypothesis are met by reality. The first part of this contribution focuses on the establishment of a comprehensive fault hypothesis for safety-critical real-time computer systems. The size of the fault containment regions, the failure mode of the fault containment regions, the assumed frequency of the faults and the assumptions about error detection latency and error containment are discussed under the premise that in future a distributed system node is expected to be a system-on-a-chip (SOC). The second part of this contribution focuses on the implications that such a fault hypothesis will have on the future architecture of distributed safety-critical real-time computer systems in the automotive domain.

Keywords: Safety-Critical Systems, Fault-Hypothesis, Error Detection, Fault-tolerance, Error-Containment, State Repair.

1 Introduction

The significant advances of the semiconductor technology in the past decades, in particular with respect to the substantial increase in the functional capabilities of chips, an incredible decrease of the production costs, and a considerable growth of the dependability per logic function makes it technically and economically attractive to replace mechanical and hydraulic control systems by computer-based control systems, even in safety-critical applications. The wide deployment of *fly-by-wire control systems* in the aerospace domain demonstrates clearly that the judicious application of computer technology can lead to an overall improvement of the safety record[1], an increase in the overall system availability and a decrease in the production and maintenance effort.

M. Broy, I.H. Krüger, and M. Meisinger (Eds.): ASWSD 2004, LNCS 4147, pp. 31–42, 2006.

It is expected that the introduction of safety-critical computer-based control systems into the automotive market (called *X-by-wire*) will eventually produce similar benefits: a significant reduction in the overall number of traffic accidents by the provision of intelligent driver assistance, a decrease of the production and development costs, and an improvement in the overall dependability of cars. Considering the failure-rate data of the available electronic components, the required level of dependability of the safety-critical control system can only be achieved if the system supports fault tolerance. The starting point for the design of a fault-tolerant system is the precise specification of a fault hypothesis at the beginning of design effort.

It is the objective of this paper to deliberate about the required contents of the fault-hypothesis for a safety-critical computer system. The paper starts with a discussion of the design challenges in safety-critical computing and reflects about the role of the fault-hypothesis in the design process. Section three is devoted to a detailed discussion of the contents of a fault-hypothesis. Section four presents a concrete example for a fault hypothesis, the fault hypothesis of the time-triggered architecture.   Section five investigates the implications that follow from this discussion for the architecture of the future control systems within a car. The paper terminates with a conclusion in Section six.

2 The Design of Safety-Critical Systems

2.1 The 10^{-9} Challenge

Ultra-dependable computer systems that are to be deployed in safety-critical applications are expected to exhibit a mean-time-to-failure (MTTF) of better than 10^9 hours[2], i.e. more than 100 000 years. Although this number has its origin in the dependability requirements of a *fly-by-wire* system, it is applicable to the automotive domain as well. It has been stipulated that the dependability requirements for a *drive-by-wire* system are even more stringent that the dependability requirements for *fly-by-wire* systems, since the number of exposed hours of humans is higher in the automotive domain.

It is *impossible* to gain confidence about a system reliability of 100 000 years by testing[3]. Thus the safety argument must be put together out of experimental data about the component reliability and analytical arguments taking into account the redundancy in the system structure, expressed in a dependability model using novel means of statistical reasoning[4].   Even a very low correlation in the failure probability of replicated subsystems has a significant effect on the system reliability of ultra-dependable systems. The system design must thus assure that replicated subsystems of an architecture for ultra-dependability systems *fail independently* of each other.

A further consequence of the *un-testability* of 10^{-9} systems is the need to analyze critical algorithms by formal methods in order to convince certification authorities of the correctness of the algorithms within the specified operational envelop. It is impossible to demonstrate solely by testing up to the required level of confidence that critical algorithms (e.g. clock synchronization, membership) are free of errors.

2.2 The Role of the Fault Hypothesis

The fault hypothesis is a statement about the assumptions made concerning the types and number of faults that a fault-tolerant system is expected to tolerate. The fault hypothesis divides the fault space into two disjoint partitions: the partition of *covered faults* and the partition of *uncovered faults[5]*. The *covered faults* are those faults that are contained in the fault-hypothesis and are addressed during the system design. The occurrence of a *covered fault* during system operation should not have an adverse effect on the availability of the *safety-critical* system functions. The occurrence of an *uncovered fault* can lead to critical system failure, since no systematic mechanisms are provided to protect against uncovered faults. During system validation it must be shown that uncovered faults are rare events.

   Before the design of a safety-critical system can commence, a precise fault hypothesis is needed for the following reasons:

   (i)   **Design of the Fault-Tolerance Algorithms:** Without a precise fault-hypothesis it is not known which fault-classes must be addressed during the system design.
   (ii) **Assumption Coverage:** There is a probability that the assumptions that are contained in the fault hypothesis are not met by reality. This probability is called the *assumption coverage[6]*. The assumption coverage predicts the probability of failure of a *perfectly designed* fault-tolerant system. Without a precise fault-hypothesis, the probability for the occurrence of uncovered faults cannot be predicted. The assumption that form the fault-hypothesis must be carefully scrutinized and in a safety-critical system it must be demonstrated that the assumption coverage is significantly better than 10^{-9}/hour.
   (iii) **Validation:** The implementation of the fault-tolerance mechanisms can only be validated, if it is precisely known which faults must be tolerated by the given system and which faults are outside the scope of the given implementation.
   (iv) **Certification:** Without a precise fault hypothesis it is impossible to certify the correct operation of a fault-tolerant system.
   (v)   **Design of the Never-Give-Up (NGU) Strategy:** In a safety-critical application, the control system may never *give up*, even if the fault-hypothesis is violated by the reality. In a properly design fault-tolerant system chances are high that a violation of the fault hypothesis is caused by a correlated shower of *external transient faults* and that a fast restart of the system after this fault shower has disappeared will be successful. The activation of the restart mechanism must be activated by a NGU algorithm. Such an NGU algorithm can only be designed if a precise fault hypothesis is available.

3 Fault Hypothesis w.r.t. Hardware Faults

In the following Section we elaborate on the required contents of a fault hypothesis w.r.t. hardware faults of a distributed real-time control system that is intended for safety-critical applications. A safety critical distributed real-time system consists of a set of node computers that are interconnected by replicated communication channels (see Figure 1).

3.1 Fault Containment Region (FCR)

The notion of a *fault-containment region (FCR)* is introduced in order to delimit the immediate impact of a *single fault* to a defined subsystem of the overall system. *A fault-containment region* is defined as the set of subsystems that share one or more common resources and that may thus be affected by a single fault. The probability of failure of two different FCRs failing at the same time should be independent, i.e., there should not be any correlation of the failure probabilities of different FCRs, Since the immediate consequences of a fault in any one of the shared resources in an FCR may impact all subsystems of the FCR, the subsystems of an FCR cannot be considered to be independent of each other and cannot be considered to form their own FCRs [7]. In the context of this paper the following shared hardware resources that can be impacted by a fault are considered:

- Computing Hardware
- Power Supply
- Timing Source
- Clock Synchronization Service
- Physical Space

For example, if two subsystems depend on a single timing source, e.g., a single oscillator or a single clock synchronization algorithm, then these two subsystems are not considered to be independent and therefore belong to the same FCR. Since this definition of independence allows that two FCRs can share the same design, e.g., the same software, design faults in the software or the hardware are not part of this fault-model.

In a distributed real-time system consisting of a set of SoCs (System on a Chip) node computers, a complete node computer must be considered to form a single FCR, since all correlated failures of two subsystems residing on the same silicon die cannot be eliminated: the subsystems residing on a single die share the same physical space, the same silicon substrate, the same manufacturing mask and manufacturing process, the same ground and power supply, probably the same timing source etc. . There is a non-negligible probability that a fault in any one of these resources will affect both subsystems simultaneously.

A communication channel connecting the nodes of the distributed system can be formed by a bus, a ring, a star or any other interconnection structure.   From the point of view of fault-containment, such a channel forms also a single FCR in a safety-critical environment.

3.2 Failure Modes

A failure mode specifies the type of failure that may occur if an FCR is impacted by a fault.   In the literature different failure modes of an FCR are introduced from *restricted* to *unrestricted*[8].   The most restricted failure mode is a *fail-silent failure*, i.e. where the assumption is made that an FCR either operates correctly or is silent.

The most unrestricted failure mode is a Byzanthine failure, where no assumptions is made about the behavior of a faulty component. Every restriction in the failure mode, i.e., every assumption about the behavior of a faulty component must be scrutinized w.r.t. the assumption coverage. It follows that a system that can tolerate an unrestricted failure mode of an FCR will lead to a better assumption coverage than a system with restricted failure modes.

Another classification considers the temporal properties of faults. We distinguish between the following five types of faults in the temporal domain:

(i)   **Transient fault:** A transient fault is caused by some random event. An example for a transient is a SEU (single event upset caused by a radioactive particle)[9].

(ii)   **Intermittent fault:** An intermittent fault is considered to be a *correlated sequence of transient faults* that is caused by some single physical degradation of a component. An example of an intermittent fault is the partial degradation of the junction of a transistor on a chip (e.g., caused by oxidation) that causes sporadic load dependent or data dependent errors. Experimental data show that an intermittent fault is likely to eventually produce a permanent fault[10].

(iii)   **Soft permanent fault:** A soft permanent fault is a corruption of the h-state or of the i-state within a component[11] without causing any permanent damage to the component. For example, a corruption can be caused by a single-even-upset (SRU)[9]. The repair of the erroneous data structure eliminates the soft-permanent fault without any further effect on the hardware.

(iv)   **Permanent fault:** A permanent fault occurs, if the hardware of an FCR brakes down permanently. An example for a permanent fault is a broken wire.

(v)   **Massive transient disturbance:** A massive transient disturbance can occur if an external event (e.g., a powerful imission of electromagnetic radiation) results in the correlated failure of two or more communication channels and possibly some of the nodes. Whereas failure mode (i) to (iv) relate to *internal* faults, failure mode (v) is concerned with an *external* fault. The probability for the occurrence of an external fault depends on the characteristics of the system environment, not on the design of the system per se.

3.3 Failure Frequency

The third part of the fault-hypothesis is concerned with the frequency of failures of the identified failure modes. Whereas a failure rate data of electronic components w.r.t. permanent failures are available in the literature[12], it is much more difficult to get consistent failures for intermittent and transient faults. One reason for this difficulty is the fact that transient failures often depend an physical location or on a particular geometry which is difficult to reproduce. For example, the SEU soft error rate caused by high-energy particles originating from the space depends on the altitude and the geographical location[9].

3.4 Error Detection Latency

The consequence of a *fault* is an *error* in the system state[8]. The time it takes to detect the error is called the *error detection latency*. The error detection latency should be very short in order to be able to process the error before it propagates to a failure that impacts parts of the system that have not been disturbed by the original fault. *Knowing that **a failure has occurred** is more important than the actual failure[13] p. 276.*

3.5 Recovery Intervals

From the point of view of reliability modeling is important to know the time it takes the system to recover from a transient fault. For a permanent fault that has not caused spare exhaustion it is important to know the time it takes until all correct FCRs have a consistent view of the faulty FCR.   For a transient fault there are thee intervals of importance

(i)   **Transient fault duration:** The time interval between the start of the transient fault and the instant when all communicating partners recognize that the transient fault has disappeared.

(ii)   **Protocol recovery interval:** The time it takes until the protocol has recovered and established a consistent view among all communicating partners (e.g., w.r.t. clock synchronization).

(iii)   **State repair interval:** The time it takes until an application has recovered from the transient fault and repaired the damage to its h-state (history state).

4 Example: The Fault Hypothesis of the TTA

The Time-Triggered Architecture (TTA) is a distributed architecture for the implementation of safety-critical applications[14].   The structure of a typical single-cluster

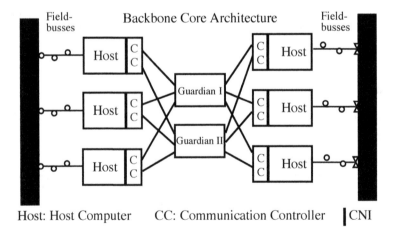

Fig. 1. Structure of the Time-Triggered Architecture

TTA system is depicted in Figure 1. Such a TTP system consists of a *backbone core architecture* of powerful node computers that are interconnected by two replicated communication channels. The media access to the communication channel is controlled by a time-division-multiple-access (TDMA) protocol. Each node computer contains a Time-Triggered Communication Controller (CC) and a host computer. The interface between the Communication Controller and the host computer is called the Communication Network Interface (CNI). A host computer can support local field-busses (e.g., CAN, LIN, or TTP/A) for the interconnection of the intelligent transducers (sensors and actuators) in the controlled object. It is a defining characteristic of the TTA that every computer has access to a fault-tolerant global time base of known precision.

In the TTA the fault hypothesis consists of the following assumptions:

(i)   A node computer forms a single FCR.

(ii)   A communication channel including the central guardian forms a single FCR.

(iii)   A node computer can fail in an arbitrary failure mode.

(iv)   A central guardian distributes the messages received from the node computers. It can fail to distribute the messages, but cannot generate messages on its own (this is called the *distribution assumption*).

(v)   The permanent failure rate of a node computer or a central guardian is in the order of 100 FIT[12] i.e. about 1000 years.

(vi)   The transient failure rate of a node computer is in the order of 100 000 FIT, i.e, about 1 year. One important mechanism that causes transient failure is an SEU [9].

(vii)   One out of about fifty failures of a node computer is *non-fail silent.* [15].

(viii) The central guardian transforms the non-fail-silent and the slightly-out-of-specification (SOS) failures of the node computers in the temporal domain to fail-silent failures in the temporal domain [16] (this is called the *SOS assumption*).

(ix)   The detection of a single error is performed by a membership algorithm. The error detection latency is less then two TDMA rounds.

(x)   The detection of multiple errors is performed by a clique avoidance algorithm. The detection latency is less than two TDMA rounds.

(xi)   The system can recover from a single transient fault within two TDMA rounds.

(xii)   The system can recover from a massive transient that destroys the clock synchronization within 8 TDMA rounds[17] after the transient has disappeared.

(xiii) The state repair time of an application takes an application specific amount of time which must be derived from knowledge about the application software.

There are two important assumptions in this fault hypothesis that must be further investigated the *distribution assumption* and the *SOS assumption*.

The distribution assumption states that the central guardian cannot distribute valid messages without having received a valid message. If the central guardian has no knowledge about how to generate a CRC of a message, the probability that a random fault will produce a random message that is syntactically correct, is generated at the proper time, is of the proper length and contains a proper CRC is far below the 10^{-9} limit.

The validity of the SOS assumption has been established by extensive fault-injection experiments[16]. In these experiments it has been shown that a central guardian provides an error-detection coverage that is above the 10^{-9} limit.

A correctly configured TTA system will recover from a massive external transient that causes correlated transient faults in the worst case *within 8 TDMA rounds* after the transient has disappeared. This scenario has been intensively investigates by using model checking[18].

At the moment the TTA implementation of TTTech [19] is in the process of being certified by the FAA (Federal Aviation Authority) for aerospace applications that are in the highest criticality class.

Considering the failure rates that have been presented above, the probability that a second independent failure will happen before the recovery from the first failure has been completed is far below the 10^{-9} limit. This is also supported by the observations from Rechtin[13] p. 277: *Chances for recovery from a **single failure** or flaw, even with complex consequences, are fairly good. Recovery from **two or more** independent failures is unlikely in real-time and uncertain in any case.*

To summarize, a properly configured TTA system tolerates a single arbitrary failure of any one of its nodes within the 10^{-9} limit.

To our knowledge there are only three computer architectures available today that tolerate the arbitrary failure of any one of its nodes, the SAFEBUS architecture[20] that is deployed in the Boeing 777 aircraft, the FTTMP architecture [21] that is used in military applications, and the TTA that is used in aerospace, railway and automotive applications.

5 Implications for the Future Architecture of Automotive Systems

What are at present the major obstacles that hinder the deployment of more advanced embedded systems within a car? We have identified five key interlinked obstacles:

(i) **Electronic Hardware Cost:** Hardware costs are recurring costs that are decisive for the economic success in a mass market. Since in today's system a new node (ECU--electronic control unit) is required for nearly every major new function, the hardware costs escalate significantly with every additional electronic function.

(ii) **Diagnosis and Maintenance:** The diagnosis of transient and intermittent component failures, which are the major cause of system outages is insufficient. For example, it has been reported in [22] that more than 50% of the supposedly failed electronic modules removed from vehicles and returned to the supplier, passed bench tests.

(iii) **Dependability:** The replacement of mechanical subsystems by electronics requires a level of electronics dependability that is higher than the dependability of the mechanical subsystems that are replaced. Such a high dependability can only be achieved by the provision of fault-tolerance. The number of physical contact points, which are a main cause of system unreliability, must be reduced.

(iv)   **Development Cost:** The unintended side effects between different application subsystems increase significantly the development and integration efforts. Changes in one subsystem often effect the operation of another subsystem. The unproductive glue code needed to support the communication of ECUs located in different networks is substantial and growing. At present the interfaces of many subsystems are ill-specified in the temporal domain [23]. As a consequence the modular certification, the reuse of software components and the ease of integration are severely compromised.

(v)   **Intellectual Property (IP) Protection:** Suppliers in the automotive supply chain are reluctant to open their IP which is contained in a compiled software module to OEMs or other suppliers in order to maintain their competitive edge.

At present the design of the electronic control system within a car is guided by the principle of *a separate box (node) for every major function*, which is characteristic for a *federated distributed architecture[24]*. What is needed is an *integrated distributed architecture* where

(i)   The number of nodes and contact points are significantly reduced by providing multiple encapsulated execution environments for disjoint distributed application subsystems (DAS) within a single physical node and within a single physical network . Examples of DASs are the subsystem for power train control, the subsystem for body electronic, or the multimedia subsystem.

(ii)   The number of cables and connectors is reduced by providing multiple *encapsulated virtual networks,* one for each subsystem, on a single physical wire.

(iii)   The arbitrary failure of any *single* node (independent of its cause) may have no serious impact on the availability of a safety-critical function.

(iv)   Generic services for strong fault isolation and fault tolerance are provided at the architecture level (by hardware supported middleware) such that different distributed application subsystems (DAS) cannot interfere unintentionally.

(v)   The precise specification of the *temporal and value properties* of interfaces is supported by the architecture in order that software can be reused without unintended side effects.

(vi)   An integrated diagnostic service that monitors, detects and diagnoses all out-of-norm conditions and transient failures in the distributed execution environment and records every anomaly of an application software module is part of the architecture.

(vii)   Standard APIs (Application Program Interfaces) that support the integration of legacy software in the form of compiled object modules are provided.

The   requirements of a fault-tolerant architecture for an integrated distributed system for safety-critical automotive applications have the following implications:

(i)   The physical structure of such a system will be primarily determined by considerations about the independence of fault-containment regions (FCR).

(ii)   Safety critical tasks must be executed in three independent FCRs and the results must be voted upon by intelligent actuators in order to tolerate any single failure of node failure (TMR structure).

(iii)   The distributed application subsystems (DAS) must be encapsulated from each other in the temporal domain and in the value domain in order to eliminate error propagation from one DAS to another DAS. This must be realized by the middleware in the node computers.

(iv)   The communication between different DAS must be realized in a controlled fashion via virtual gateways.

(v)   The physical communication channel between the backbone nodes of Figure 1 should support a number of encapsulated virtual channels in parallel in order to minimize the cabling points, a major source of failure. Each DAS will have its own virtual channel (e.g., a virtual CAN) that spans a number of physical communication links.

(vi)   Diagnostics must be an integral service of the architecture. It is important to distinguish between diagnostics of the distributed computer system per se and diagnostics of the DASs which includes the diagnostics of the sensors and actuators. The diagnostics of the distributed computer system (e.g., a distributed membership service) should be provided by the base architecture with minimal involvement of the applications. This separation of the diagnostics effort is necessary, because *the cost to find and **fix** an inadequate or failed part increases by an **order of magnitude** as it is successively incorporated into higher levels in the system[13]p. 276.*

(vii)   It must be possible to introduce a new generation of processing hardware and communication channels without a major impact on the operation of legacy applications. In other words, it must be possible to change the hardware without having to modify the application software in order to be able to take advantage of new hardware developments promptly.

With the generous support from the European Community in the context of the FP 6 DECOS project proposal we plan to develop such an integrated architecture on top of the existing and proven TTA in cooperation with major companies from the automotive, the railway and the control industries.

6 Conclusions

The fault hypothesis states the assumptions about the types and number of faults that a fault-tolerant system must tolerate. The fault-hypothesis must be established at the beginning of the design process, since it has a profound influence on the architecture of the emerging fault-tolerant system. It is thus the most important document for the design process. Without a precise fault hypothesis it is impossible to decide which faults are *covered* and which faults are *uncovered* by a given design. In order to achieve a high *assumption coverage* the fault hypothesis should make minimal assumptions about the *behavior of faulty nodes*. These minimal assumptions must be carefully scrutinized in order to establish that the *assumption coverage* is in agreement with the overall dependability objective of the intended system.

Acknowledgements

This work has been supported, in part by the European IST project *NEXT TTA* and by the IST Integrated Project *DECOS.*

References

1. Phillips, D., *Major US Airlines Complete Safest Year*, in *Washington Post, June 13, 2003, p. A10.* 2003.
2. Suri, N., C.J. Walter, and M.M. Hugue, eds. *Advances in Ultra-Dependable Systems.* 1995, IEEE Press.
3. Littlewood, B. and L. Strigini, *Validation of Ultra-high Dependability for Software-based Systems.* Communications of the ACM, 1993. **36**(11): p. 69-80.
4. Kaufman, L.F., B.W. Johnson, and J.B. Dugan, *Coverage Estimtion Using Statistics of the Extremes for When Testing Reveals No Failures.* IEEE Trans. on Computers, 2002. **51**(1): p. 3-12.
5. Hugue, M.M. and R. Scalzo. *Specifying fault-tolerance in large complex computing systems.* in *Engineering of Complex Computer Systems.* 1995. Fr. Lauderdale Florida: IEEE Press.
6. Powell, D. *Failure Mode Assumptions and Assumption Coverage.* in *Proc. 22nd Int. Symp. on Fault-Tolerant Computing (FTCS-22).* 1992. Boston, MA, USA: IEEE Computer Society Press.
7. Kaufmann, L.F., S. B., and B.W. Johnson. *Modeling of Common-Mode Failures in Digital Embedded Systems.* in *Proc. of the Reliability and Maintainability Symposium 2000.* 2000. Los Angeles, Cal.: IEEE Press.
8. Laprie, J.C., ed. *Dependability: Basic Concepts and Terminology - in English, French, German, German and Japanese.* Dependable Computing and Fault Tolerance, ed. A. Avizienis, H. Kopetz, and J.-C. Laprie. Vol. 5. 1992, Springer-Verlag: Vienna, Austria.
9. Normand, E., *Single Event Upset at Ground Level.* IEEETrans. on Nucl. Science,, 1996. **43**: p. 2742.
10. Constantinescu, C. *Impact of Deep Submicron Technology on Dependability of VLSI Circuits.* in *Proc. of the 2002 International Conference on Dependable Systems and Networks.* 2002. Washington D.C.: IEEE Press.
11. Kopetz, H., *Real-Time Systems, Design Principles for Distributed Embedded Applications; ISBN: 0-7923-9894-7, Seventh printing 2003.* 1997, Boston: Kluwer Academic Publishers.
12. Pauli, B., A. Meyna, and P. Heitmann, *Reliability of Electronic Components and Control Units in Motor Vehicle Applications.* 1998, Verein Deutscher Ingenieure (VDI). p. 1009-1024.
13. Rechtin, E. and M.W. Maier, *The Art of Systems Architecting.* 2002, Boca Raton, USA: CRC Press. 313.
14. Kopetz, H. and G. Bauer, *The Time-Triggered Architecture.* Proceedings of the IEEE, 2003. **91**(January 2003): p. 112-126.
15. Karlsson, J., et al., *Integration and Comparison of Three Physical Fault Injection Techniques*, in *Predictably Dependable Computing Systems*, B. Randell, et al., Editors. 1995, Springer Verlag: Heidelberg. p. 309-327.
16. Ademaj, A., et al. *Dependability Evaluation of the Time-Triggered Architecture with Bus and Star Topology.* in *DSN Conference.* 2003. San Francisco: IEEE Press.

17. Steiner, W., M. Paulitsch, and H. Kopetz. *Multiple Failure Correction in the Time-Triggered Architecture*. in *Proc. of the IEEE WORDS 2003 Conference*. 2003. CAPRI, Italy: IEEE Press.
18. Steiner, W., J. Rushby, and H. Pfeifer, *xxx*. 2003.
19. TTTech, *homepage of TTTech at www.tttech.com*. 1998.
20. Driscoll, K. and K. Hoyme, *SafeBus for avionics*. IEEE Aerospace and Electronics Systems Magazine, 1993. **8**(3): p. 34-39.
21. Lala, J.H. and L.S. Alger. *Hardware and Software Fault Tolerance: A unified architectural approach*. in *Proc. 18th Int. Symp. on Fault-Tolerant Computing (FTCS-18)*. 1988. Tokyo.
22. Kimseng , K., et al., *Physics-of-failure assessment of a cruise control module*. Microelectronics Reliability, 1999. **39**: p. 1423-1444.
23. Kopetz, H. and N. Suri. *Compositional Design of Real-Time System: A Conceptual Basis for the Specification of Linking Interfaces*. in *ISORC 2003--The 6th International Symposium on Object Oriented Real-Time Computing*. 2003. Hakodate, Japan: IEEE Press.
24. Swanson, D.L. *Evolving Avionics Systems for Federated to Distributed Architectures*. in *Proc. of the 17th Digital Avionics System Conference*. 1998: IEEE Press.

A Compositional Framework for Real-Time Guarantees*

Insik Shin and Insup Lee

Departement of Computer and Information Science
University of Pennsylvania
Philadelphia PA 19104, USA

Abstract. Our primary goal is to develop a compositional real-time scheduling framework where global (system-level) timing properties are established by composing together independently (specified and) analyzed local (component-level) timing properties. In this paper, we define two problems and one design issue in developing such a framework and present our approaches to the problems and the design issue. The two problems are (1) the scheduling interface derivation problem that is to (exactly) abstract the collective real-time requirements of a component as a single real-time requirement, or a scheduling interface and (2) the scheduling interface composition problem that is to (exactly) compose the scheduling interfaces of components into the system-level scheduling interface. The design issue is how to define a scheduling interface model. Our approach is to use the standard periodic model as the scheduling interface model and to address the two problems with the periodic model. We introduce exact conditions under which our proposed periodic scheduling interface model can abstract the collective real-time requirements that a set of periodic tasks demands under EDF (earliest deadline first) and RM (rate monotonic) scheduling. We present simulation results to evaluate the overheads that the periodic scheduling interfaces incur in terms of utilization increase.

1 Introduction

As embedded systems become more complex due to increased functionalities, it is necessary to develop techniques and methods that facilitate the designing of large complex systems from subsystems. Component technology has been widely accepted as a methodology for designing large complex systems through systematic abstractions. Component-based design provides a means for decomposing a system into components, allowing the reduction of a single complex design problem into multiple simpler design problems, and for composing components into a system through component interfaces that abstract and hide their internal complexity. Component-based design also facilitates the reuse of components that may have been developed in different environments. A central idea in component-based design is to compose components into a larger system with the proper

---

* This research was supported in part by NSF CCR-9988409, NSF CCR-0086147, NSF CCR-0209024, ARO DAAD19-01-1-0473, and ETRI.

M. Broy, I.H. Krüger, and M. Meisinger (Eds.): ASWSD 2004, LNCS 4147, pp. 43–56, 2006.
© Springer-Verlag Berlin Heidelberg 2006

notion of *compositionality* such that properties that have been established at the component level also hold at the system level. To preserve compositionality, the properties of the larger component need to abstract the collective properties of smaller components. There has been much work in how to define interfaces for components to ensure composability. Traditionally, interface has emphasis on syntactic convention and type information. Lately, there has been a spate of effort to include behavioral and functional information as part of interface definitions. These approaches focus on ways to specify behavioral and functional aspects of components and how to check statically the consistency of composed components.

For embedded systems that are also real-time systems, it is important that timing guarantees at the component level can be analyzed compositionally as components are combined hierarchically. When the timing properties of components can be analyzed compositionally, component-based real-time systems allow components to be developed and validated independently and to be assembled together without revalidating the whole system. In the real-time systems research, there has been a growing attention to hierarchical scheduling frameworks where components (applications) form a hierarchy [4,7,9,5,13,14,10,15]. Many studies [4,7,9,5,13,14] introduced methods to analyze the schedulability of a component in a hierarchical scheduling framework. However, few studies addressed the problem of preserving compositionality in hierarchical schedulability analysis. Recently, two studies [10,15] began to address the problem of analyzing the timing properties of components compositionally. This paper extends these initial results [10,15], and mainly clarifies and addresses the problem of preserving compositionality on timing properties in component-based real-time systems.

Our primary goal is to develop a compositional real-time scheduling framework where global (system level) timing properties are established by composing together independently (specified and) analyzed local (component level) timing properties. To develop such a framework, the following two problems need to be addressed. (1) The *scheduling interface derivation* problem is to combine and abstract the collective real-time requirements of a component as a single real-time requirement, called *scheduling interface*. (2) The *scheduling interface composition* problem is to compose independently analyzed local timing properties under their local schedulers into a global timing property under a global scheduler.

In a compositional real-time scheduling framework, the major issue is how to define a *scheduling interface model* in order to specify the collective real-time requirements of a component. Our approach is to use the standard Liu and Layland periodic model [11] as a scheduling interface model to develop a compositional real-time scheduling framework. Then, we address the scheduling interface derivation problem by abstracting a set of periodic tasks under EDF or RM scheduling as a periodic scheduling interface. When a component exports its periodic scheduling interface to the system, the system can thus treat the component as a single periodic task. Using the same technique as for the scheduling interface derivation problem, we address the scheduling interface composition problem by composing a set of periodic interfaces under EDF or RM scheduling as a single periodic interface. Thus, the global timing property can be established by composing periodic scheduling interfaces as a single periodic scheduling interface.

The rest of the paper is organized as follows. Section 2 presents an overview of a compositional real-time scheduling framework and the models of our framework. Section 3 introduces a periodic resource model, and Section 4 provides exact schedulability conditions for a scheduling component with the periodic resource model. Section 5 addresses the scheduling interface derivation and composition problems using the periodic resource model as a scheduling interface model, and Section 6 evaluates the overheads that the periodic scheduling interface incurs in terms of utilization increase through simulations. Section 7 presents related work, and Section 8 concludes with discussion on future research.

2   Compositional Framework Overview and Models

In this section, we first present an overview of a compositional scheduling framework without regards to any specific models and then provide the specific models that we use to develop such a compositional scheduling framework.

2.1   Compositional Framework Overview

We consider a *compositional scheduling framework*, where scheduling components form a hierarchy and a resource is allocated from a parent component to its child components in the hierarchy. A *scheduling component* is the basic unit of scheduling. Scheduling is to assign resources according to scheduling algorithm in order to service workloads. We define a scheduling component C as a triple (W, R, A), where W describes the workloads (of applications) supported in the scheduling component, R is a resource model that describes the resource allocations available to the scheduling component, and A is a scheduling algorithm which describes how the workloads share the resources at all times.

The *resource demand* of a component $C(W, R, A)$ represents the collective resource requirements that its workload set W requests under its scheduling algorithm A. The *demand bound function* $\mathrm{dbf}_A(W, t)$ of a component $C(W, R, A)$ calculates the maximum possible resource demands that W requests under A for a time interval of length t. The *resource supply* of a resource R represents the amount of resource allocations that R provides. The *supply bound function* $\mathrm{sbf}_R(t)$ of a resource R calculates the minimum possible resource supplies that R provides during a time interval of length t. A resource R is said to *satisfy* a resource demand of W under A if $\mathrm{dbf}_A(W, t) \leq \mathrm{sbf}_R(t)$ for all interval length t.

A component $C(W, R, A)$ is said to be *schedulable* if its resource supply satisfies its resource demand. That is, a scheduling component C is schedulable if a workload set W is schedulable under a scheduling algorithm A over the minimum possible resource supply of a resource R. We define a *scheduling interface derivation* problem as follows: given a workload set W and a scheduling algorithm A, the problem is to find a resource R, or a scheduling interface R, such that a scheduling component $C(W, R, A)$ is schedulable. The scheduling interface derivation problem may have some additional constraints such as minimizing the resource capacity requirement of R and/or minimizing the context switch overheads.

In a hierarchy of scheduling components, a parent component provides resource allocations to its child components. Once a child component C_1 finds a scheduling interface R_1, it exports the scheduling interface R_1 to its parent component. The parent component treats the scheduling interface R_1 as a single workload model T_1. As long as the parent component satisfies the resource requirements imposed by the single workload model T_1, the parent component is able to satisfy the resource demand of a child component C_1. This scheme makes it possible for a parent component to supply resources to its child components without controlling (or even understanding) how the child components schedule resources for their own various independent tasks.

Now, we consider a *scheduling interface composition* problem as follows: given two pairs of a workload set and a scheduling algorithm, (W_1, A_1) and (W_2, A_2), and one additional scheduling algorithm A, the problem is to find R, R_1, and R_2 such that a scheduling component $C(W, R, A)$, where $W = \{R_1, R_2\}$, is schedulable, if and only if, two scheduling components $C_1(W_1, R_1, A_1)$ and $C_2(W_2, R_2, A_2)$ are schedulable.

2.2   Compositional Framework Models

We now present the specific models used in our compositional scheduling framework.

As a workload model in our framework, we consider the standard Liu and Layland periodic task model $T(p, e)$, where p is a period and e is an execution time requirement [11]. A task utilization U_T is defined as e/p. For a workload set $W = \{T_i\}$, a workload utilization U_W is defined as $\sum_{T_i \in W} U_{T_i}$. We consider that all tasks in a component are synchronous, i.e., they release their initial jobs at the same time. We assume that each task is independent and preemptive.

As a scheduling algorithm, we consider the earliest deadline first (EDF) algorithm, an optimal dynamic scheduling algorithm [11], and the rate monotonic (RM) algorithm, an optimal fixed-priority scheduling algorithm [11].

Resources can fall into two categories depending on whether they are exclusively allocated to a single scheduling component or they are shared by multiple scheduling components, i.e.,

- *Dedicated Resource*: A resource is said to be dedicated if it is available to a single scheduling component at all times at its full capacity.
- *Shared Resource*: A resource is said to be shared if it is not a dedicated resource. Depending on resource sharing nature, we can also classify shared resources as follows:
  - *Fractional Resource*: A resource is said to be fractional if it is available to a scheduling component at all times but at a fractional capacity. A fractional resource is a shared resource on the basis of capacity-sharing or General-Processor-Sharing (GPS) [12].

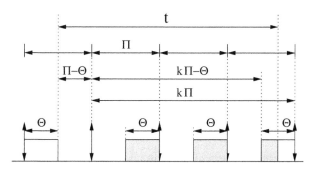

Fig. 1. The supply bound function of a periodic resource model $\Gamma(\Pi, \Theta)$ for $k = 3$; the figure shows a worst-case scenario, where $\Gamma(\Pi, \Theta)$ provides the minimum possible resource supply (represented as gray boxes) during an interval of length t

- *Partitioned Resource*: A resource is said to be partitioned if it is available to a scheduling component at some times at its full capacity but not available at all at the other times. A partitioned resource is a shared resource on the basis of time-sharing. In our framework, we consider partitioned (time-sharing) resources such as CPU and network bandwidth.

As a resource model, we consider a periodic resource model $\Gamma(\Pi, \Theta)$ that we proposed in our earlier work [15].

As a scheduling interface model, we consider the periodic resource model.

3   Periodic Resource Model

A resource model is important in a compositional scheduling framework, since it constitutes a method that enables the schedulability of a component to be analyzed independently, and thus it can be used as a scheduling interface model. In this section, we briefly review an existing periodic resource model.

We proposed a periodic resource model $\Gamma(\Pi, \Theta)$ [15], where Π is a period ($\Pi > 0$) and Θ is a periodic allocation time ($0 < \Theta \le \Pi$). A resource capacity C_Γ of a periodic resource $\Gamma(\Pi, \Theta)$ is Θ/Π. This periodic model $\Gamma(\Pi, \Theta)$ is defined to characterize the following property:

$$\text{supply}_\Gamma\big(k\Pi, (k+1)\Pi\big) = \Theta, \quad \text{where } k = 0, 1, 2, \ldots. \tag{1}$$

For schedulability analysis, it is important to calculate the minimum resource supply of a resource model accurately. For a periodic model Γ, its supply bound function $\text{sbf}_\Gamma(t)$ is defined to compute the minimum resource supply for every interval length t as follows:

$$\text{sbf}_\Gamma(t) = \begin{cases} t - (k+1)(\Pi - \Theta) & \text{if } t \in [(k+1)\Pi - 2\Theta, (k+1)\Pi - \Theta], \\ (k-1)\Theta & \text{otherwise,} \end{cases} \tag{2}$$

where $k = \max\left(\lceil (t - (\Pi - \Theta))/\Pi \rceil, 1\right)$. Figure 1 illustrates how the supply bound function $\text{sbf}_\Gamma(t)$ is defined.

Since the supply bound function $\mathtt{sbf}_\Gamma(t)$ is a discrete function, its linear lower bound function $\mathtt{lsbf}_\Gamma(t)$ is defined as follows:

$$\mathtt{lsbf}_\Gamma(t) = \begin{cases} \frac{\Theta}{\Pi}\left(t - 2(\Pi - \Theta)\right) & \text{if } (t \geq 2(\Pi - \Theta)), \\ 0 & \text{otherwise.} \end{cases} \tag{3}$$

4   Schedulability Analysis of Scheduling Component

Our primary concern is to establish a global system schedulability property by composing local component schedulability properties that are independently analyzed. In our earlier work [15], we presented conditions under which the schedulability of a component can be exactly analyzed independently under EDF and fixed-priority scheduling. In this section, we provide the schedulability conditions of a scheduling component and illustrate a schedulability region of the scheduling component.

4.1   Schedulability Analysis Under EDF Scheduling

For a periodic task set W under EDF scheduling, Baruah et al. [1] proposed a *demand bound function* that computes the total resource demand $\mathtt{dbf}_{\mathsf{EDF}}(W, t)$ of W for every interval length t.

$$\mathtt{dbf}_{\mathsf{EDF}}(W, t) = \sum_{T_i \in W} \left\lfloor \frac{t}{p_i} \right\rfloor \cdot e_i, \tag{4}$$

where p_i is the period of task T_i and e_i is the execution time requirement of T_i.

We present the following theorem to provide an exact condition under which the schedulability of a component $C(W, R, \mathsf{EDF})$ can be analyzed for any partitioned resource R.

Theorem 1. *A scheduling component $C(W, R, A)$ is schedulable, where $A = \mathsf{EDF}$, if and only if*

$$\forall 0 < t \leq LCM_W \quad \mathtt{dbf}_{\mathsf{EDF}}(W, t) \leq \mathtt{sbf}_\Gamma(t), \tag{5}$$

where LCM_W is the least common multiple of p_i for all $T_i \in W$.

Proof. To show the necessity, we prove the contrapositive, i.e., if Eq. (5) is false, all workload members of W are not schedulable by EDF. If the total resource demand of W under EDF scheduling during t exceeds the total resource supply provided by R during t, there is clearly no feasible schedule.

To show the sufficiency, we prove the contrapositive, i.e., if all workload members of W are not schedulable by EDF, then Eq. (5) is false. Let t_2 be the first instant at which a job of some workload member T_i of W that misses its deadline. Let t_1 be the latest instant at which the resource supplied to W was idle or was executing a job whose deadline is after t_2. By the definition of t_1, there is a job whose deadline is before t_2 was released at t_1. Without loss of generality, we

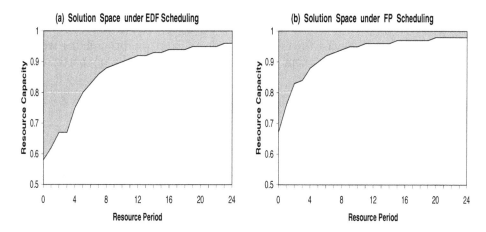

Fig. 2. Schedulable region of a periodic resource $\Gamma(\Pi, \Theta)$: (a) under EDF scheduling and (b) under fixed-priority (FP) scheduling

can assume that $t = t_2 - t_1$. Since T_i misses its deadline at t_2, the total demand placed on W in the time interval $[t_1, t_2)$ is greater than the total supply provided by R in the same time interval length t.

As an example, let us consider a workload set $W = \{T_1(3, 1), T_2(4, 1)\}$ and a scheduling algorithm $A = \mathsf{EDF}$. The workload utilization U_W is 0.58. In Figure 2(a), the gray area shows a solution space of a periodic resource $\Gamma(\Pi, \Theta)$ for the problem of guaranteeing the schedulability of this example component $C(W, \Gamma, \mathsf{EDF})$. To obtain such a solution space of $\Gamma(\Pi, \Theta)$, we computed the minimum periodic resource capacity C_Γ^* for each integer resource period $\Pi = 1, \ldots, 24$ such that the example component $C(W, \Gamma(\Pi, \Theta), \mathsf{EDF})$ is schedulable according to Theorem 1 if $C_\Gamma \geq C_\Gamma^*$. For instance, the minimum periodic resource capacity for the schedulability of the example component is 0.67 when a resource period Π is 2. Thus, a periodic resource $\Gamma(2, 1.40)$, which is in the gray area, guarantees the schedulability of the example component $C(W, \Gamma(2, 1.40), \mathsf{EDF})$.

4.2   Schedulability Analysis Under Fixed-Priority Scheduling

For a periodic task set W under fixed-priority (FP) scheduling, Lehoczky et al. [8] proposed a demand bound function $\mathsf{dbf}_{\mathsf{FP}}(W, t, i)$ that computes the worst-case cumulative resource demand of a task T_i for an interval of length t.

$$\mathsf{dbf}_{\mathsf{FP}}(W, t, i) = e_i + \sum_{T_k \in \mathsf{HP}_W(i)} \left\lceil \frac{t}{p_k} \right\rceil \cdot e_k,$$

where $\mathsf{HP}_W(i)$ is a set of higher-priority tasks than T_i in W and p_i and e_i are the period and the execution time requirement of T_i, respectively.

For a task T_i over a resource R, the worst-case response time $r_i(R)$ of T_i can be computed as follows:

$$r_i(R) = \min\{t\} \quad \text{such that} \quad \mathsf{dbf_{FP}}(W, t, i) \leq \mathsf{sbf}_\Gamma(t).$$

We present the following theorem to provide an exact condition under which the schedulability of a component $C(W, R, \mathsf{FP})$ is guaranteed for any partitioned resource R.

Theorem 2. *A scheduling component $C(W, R, A)$ is schedulable, where $A = \mathsf{FP}$, if and only if*

$$\forall T_i \in W \quad \exists t_i \in [0, p_i] \quad \mathsf{dbf_{FP}}(W, t_i, i) \leq \mathsf{sbf}_\Gamma(t_i).$$

Proof. Task T_i completes its execution requirement at time $t \in [0, p_i]$, if and only if e_i, the execution requirement of T_i, plus all the execution requirements from all the jobs of higher-priority tasks than T_i are completed at time t.

The total of such requirements is given by $\mathsf{dbf_{FP}}(W, t, i)$, and they are completed at t if and only if $\mathsf{dbf_{FP}}(W, t_i, i) = \mathsf{sbf}_\Gamma(t_i)$ and $\mathsf{dbf_{FP}}(W, t_i', i) > \mathsf{sbf}_\Gamma(t_i')$ for $0 \leq t_i' < t_i$. It follows that a necessary and sufficient condition for T_i to meet its deadline is the existence of a $t_i \in [0, p_i]$ such that $\mathsf{dbf_{FP}}(W, t_i, i) = \mathsf{sbf}_\Gamma(t_i)$.

The entire task set is schedulable if and only if each of the tasks is schedulable. This means that there exists a $t_i \in [0, p_i]$ such that $\mathsf{dbf_{FP}}(W, t_i, i) = \mathsf{sbf}_\Gamma(t_i)$ for each task $T_i \in W$.

As an example, let us consider a workload set $W = \{T_1(3, 1), T_2(4, 1)\}$ and a scheduling algorithm $A = \mathsf{FP}$. In Figure 2(b), the gray area shows a solution space of a periodic resource $\Gamma(\Pi, \Theta)$ for the problem of guaranteeing the schedulability of this example component $C(W, \Gamma, \mathsf{FP})$. To obtain such a solution space, we computed the minimum periodic resource capacity C_Γ^* for each integer resource period $\Pi = 1, \ldots, 24$ such that the example component $C(W, \Gamma, \mathsf{FP})$ is schedulable according to Theorem 2 if $C_\Gamma \geq C_\Gamma^*$. For instance, the minimum periodic resource capacity for the schedulability of the example component is 0.83 when a resource period Π is 2. Thus, a periodic resource $\Gamma(2, 1.80)$, which is in the gray area, guarantees the schedulability of the example component $C(W, \Gamma(2, 1.80), \mathsf{FP})$.

5   Scheduling Interface Derivation and Composition

In this section, we address the problem of abstracting the collective resource requirements of a component into a single scheduling interface model. We define the scheduling interface derivation problem as follows: given a workload set $W = \{T_1, \ldots, T_n\}$ and a scheduling algorithm $A = EDF/RM$, the problem is to find a periodic resource model $\Gamma(\Pi, \Theta)$ such that $C(W, \Gamma, A)$ is schedulable and the resource capacity C_Γ of Γ is minimized.

We define a method, called comp, that finds a solution to the scheduling interface derivation problem assuming that the range of a resource period Π is given, i.e., $\Pi \in [\Pi_{min}, \Pi_{max}]$. The comp method employs an exhaustive search to find the solution $\Gamma(\Pi, \Theta)$ using Theorem 1 for EDF scheduling or Theorem 2 for RM scheduling depending on $A = EDF$ or RM. As a technique to implement the exhaustive search to find a solution, one can use a binary search starting from a point $\Gamma(\Pi, \Theta)$ such that $C_\Gamma = U_W$.

Once a child component finds a solution $\Gamma(\Pi, \Theta)$ to the scheduling interface derivation problem, it exports the solution to its parent component. The parent component treats the periodic resource model $\Gamma(\Pi, \Theta)$ as a standard periodic task model $T(p, e)$, where $p = \Pi$ and $e = \Theta$. This scheme makes it possible for a parent component to supply resources to its child components without controlling (or even understanding) how the child components schedule resources for their own various independent tasks.

As an example, let us consider a workload set $W = \{T_1(3, 1), T_2(4, 1), T_3(5, 1)\}$ and a scheduling algorithm $A = EDF$. Now, we consider finding a periodic resource model $\Gamma(\Pi, \Theta)$ as a solution to the component abstraction problem with a resource period constraint of $\Pi \in [2, 5]$. The comp method finds a periodic resource model $\Gamma(2, 1.59)$ as the solution to the problem in a sense that $\Gamma(2, 1.59)$ has the minimum resource capacity while satisfying the schedulability constraint of $C(W, \Gamma, EDF)$ and the resource period constraint.

Since a periodic scheduling interface model is identical to a periodic task model, the scheduling interface composition problem can be addressed by the same solution as for the scheduling interface derivation problem.

6   Evaluations of Component Abstraction Overheads

We performed simulations to evaluate the overheads that solutions to scheduling interface derivation problems incur in terms of utilization increase.

6.1   Simulation Settings

In all simulations, our performance measure is the overhead of a component abstraction in terms of utilization increase. Let Γ be a solution that the comp finds to the component abstraction problem of a component $C(W, \Gamma, A)$. The *component abstraction overhead* $O(\Gamma)$ of Γ is defined as

$$O(\Gamma) = \frac{C_\Gamma - U_W}{U_W}, \quad \text{where } C(W, \Gamma, A) \text{ is schedulable.} \tag{6}$$

During simulations, we have the following simulation parameters:

- Workload Size ($|W|$): The number of tasks in the workload W is $10, 20, \ldots, 80$.
- Workload Utilization (U_W) : The utilization of the workload W is in the range $[0.1, 0.8]$
- Task Model $T(p, e)$: Each task T has a period p randomly generated in the range $[100, 1000]$ and an execution time e randomly generated in the range $[1, p/3]$.
- Scheduling Algorithm (A) : A is EDF or RM.
- Resource Period (Π) : The period of a periodic resource is in the range $[1, 180]$.

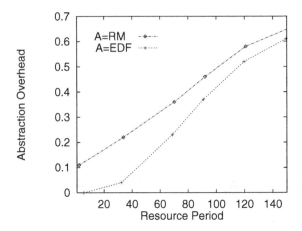

Fig. 3. Component abstraction overhead as a function of resource period

6.2   Simulation Results

Figure 3 shows the effect of a resource period on the average component abstraction overheads. With the simulation settings of $|W| = 20$, $U_W \in [0.4, 0.6]$, and $A = EDF/RM$, we ran 1000 simulation runs to get each point in the graphs. During the simulations, we have 6 resource period ranges $[30k + 1, 30(k + 1)]$, where $k = 0, 1, \ldots, 5$. Each point in the graphs represents a resource period that minimizes the component abstraction overhead during the resource period range of $[30k + 1, 30(k + 1)]$. Figure 3 shows that the resource period has a significant effect on the average component abstraction overheads for both EDF and RM scheduling algorithms. The results show that it is advantageous to have a smaller resource period for a periodic scheduling interface.

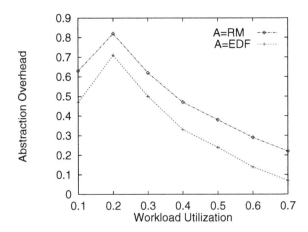

Fig. 4. Component abstraction overhead as a function of workload utilization

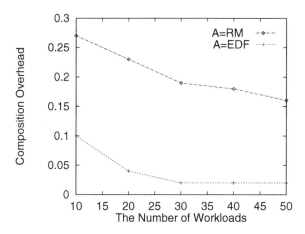

Fig. 5. Component abstraction overhead as a function of the number of tasks

Figure 4 shows the effect of the workload utilization of a component on the average component abstraction overhead. With the simulation settings of $|W| = 20$, $\Pi \in [61, 90]$, and $A = EDF/RM$, 1000 simulation runs were performed. Figure 4 shows that the average component abstraction overhead is considerable when the workload utilization is very small, i.e., less than 0.3. However, the results show that the component abstraction overhead issue seems less significant when the workload utilization get higher.

Figure 5 shows the effect of the number of tasks in a component on the average component abstraction overhead. With the simulation settings of $U_W = 0.50$ and $\Pi \in [61, 90]$, we ran at least 300 simulation runs when $A = EDF$ and 1000 simulation runs when $A = RM$ to obtain each point in the graphs. Figure 5 shows that the effect of the workload size becomes a bit more significant when it gets smaller. Thus, we can see that the periodic scheduling interfaces seem to be more efficiently derived when a component has a larger number of tasks.

7   Related Work

In the real-time systems research, there is a growing attention to hierarchical scheduling frameworks [4,7,9,5,13,14,10,15] that support hierarchical resource sharing under different scheduling algorithms.

Deng and Liu [4] introduced a two-level hierarchical scheduling framework where each component (application) can have any scheduler to schedule its tasks while the system has only the EDF scheduler to schedule components. For such a framework, Lipari and Baruah [9] presented exact schedulability conditions, assuming the system scheduler has knowledge of the task-level deadlines of each component. An implicit assumption on their schedulability analysis is that each component is given a fractional resource from the system scheduler. Kuo and Li [7] showed that the RM scheduler can be used as the system scheduler, only when all periodic tasks across components are harmonic. None of these study addressed the scheduling interface derivation and composition problems.

Feng and Mok [5] proposed a bounded-delay resource model to describe a partitioned resource in a hierarchical scheduling framework. Their model can be used to specify the real-time guarantees that a parent component provides to its child components while any scheduler can work in the parent component as well as in the child components. For their framework where a parent component and their child components are cleanly separated, they presented a sufficient schedulability condition. For a case where a child component has a fixed-priority scheduler, Saewong et al. [14] presented a schedulability analysis based on the worst-case response time calculations. These studies did not address the scheduling interface derivation and composition problems.

Lipari and Bini [10] and Shin and Lee [15] considered a periodic resource model for a compositional hierarchical scheduling framework. Their periodic resource model describes a behavior of a periodic resource and calculates its minimum resource allocations. For a hierarchical scheduling framework where each component can have any scheduler, they presented exact schedulability conditions such that a component is schedulable if and only if its maximum resource demand is no greater than the minimum resource supply given to the component.[1] Based on this schedulability analysis, they both considered the problem of composing the collective real-time requirements of a component into a single real-time requirement by their periodic resource model. This paper extends these initial studies by clearly defining a compositional scheduling framework and investigating the overheads that periodic scheduling interfaces incur in terms of utilization increase.

Regehr and Stankovic [13] introduced another hierarchical scheduling framework that considers various kinds of real-time guarantees. Their work focused on converting one kind of guarantee to another kind of guarantee such that whenever the former is satisfied, the latter is satisfied. With their conversion rules, the schedulability of the child component is sufficiently analyzed such that it is schedulable if its parent component provides real-time guarantees that can be converted to the real-time guarantee that the child component demands. They assumed it is given the real-time guarantee which a child component demands and did not consider the problem of deriving the real-time demands from the child component, which we address in this paper.

Chakrabarti et al. [3] proposed a formal notion of component interface to abstract resource consuming information. Their resource interface models a component through a control flow graph whose states quantify the amount of resource consumption such as memory use and power consumption. This work focuses on providing a formalism that computes the amount of resource consumption when components are assembled, while our work focuses on providing a formal technique that combines a set of temporal resource requirements into a single

---

[1] Lipari and Bini presented their schedulability condition as a sufficient condition. However, we consider it as an exact condition based on a different notion of schedulability.

temporal requirement when components are assembled. We believe that their framework and our framework can be combined to develop resource interfaces that expose the quantitative and temporal aspects of resource consumption of a component.

8   Conclusion

In this paper, we clearly defined the problems to develop a compositional real-time scheduling framework and presented our approaches to the problems. We believe that our periodic scheduling interface model can be used to abstract the temporal behavior of embedded (automotive) software components. Since much of automotive systems are real-time, the compositional property of the scheduling component should facilitate the interoperability of components that are developed separately with respect to timing constraints.

In this paper, we consider a scheduling interface model for hard real-time component-based systems. Our future work includes extending our framework for soft real-time component-based systems. This raises the issues of developing soft real-time scheduling interface models. Soft real-time task models such as the (m, k)-firm deadline model [6] and the weakly hard task model [2] can be useful to develop scheduling interface models for compositional soft real-time scheduling framework. In this paper, we assume that each task is independent. However, tasks may interact with each other through communications and synchronizations. We also consider extending our framework to deal with this issue.

References

1. S. Baruah, A. Mok, and L. Rosier. Preemptively scheduling hard-real-time sporadic tasks on one processor. In *Proc. of IEEE Real-Time Systems Symposium*, pages 182–190, December 1990.
2. G. Bernat, A. Burns, and A Llamosi. Weakly hard real-time systems. *IEEE Transactions on Computers*, 50(4):308–321, 2001.
3. A. Chakrabarti, L. de Alfaro, T. A. Henzinger, and M. Stoelinga. Resource interfaces. In *Proceedings of the Third International Conference on Embedded Software (EMSOFT)*. Lecture Notes in Computer Science, Springer-Verlag, 2003.
4. Z. Deng and J. W.-S. Liu. Scheduling real-time applications in an open environment. In *Proc. of IEEE Real-Time Systems Symposium*, pages 308–319, December 1997.
5. X. Feng and A. Mok. A model of hierarchical real-time virtual resources. In *Proc. of IEEE Real-Time Systems Symposium*, pages 26–35, December 2002.
6. M. Hamdaoui and P. Ramanathan. A dynamic priority assignment technique for streams with (m, k)-firm deadlines. *IEEE Transactions on Computers*, 44(12): 1443–1451, 1995.
7. T.-W. Kuo and C.H. Li. A fixed-priority-driven open environment for real-time applications. In *Proc. of IEEE Real-Time Systems Symposium*, pages 256–267, December 1999.

8. J. Lehoczky, L. Sha, and Y. Ding. The rate monotonic scheduling algorithm: exact characterization and average case behavior. In *Proc. of IEEE Real-Time Systems Symposium*, pages 166–171, 1989.

9. G. Lipari and S. Baruah. A hierarchical extension to the constant bandwidth server framework. In *Proc. of IEEE Real-Time Technology and Applications Symposium*, pages 26–35, May 2001.

10. G. Lipari and E. Bini. Resource partitioning among real-time applications. In *Proc. of Euromicro Conference on Real-Time Systems*, July 2003.

11. C.L. Liu and J.W. Layland. Scheduling algorithms for multi-programming in a hard-real-time environment. *Journal of the ACM*, 20(1):46 – 61, 1973.

12. A. K. Parekh and R. G. Gallagher. A generalized processor sharing approach to flow control in integrated services networks: the single-node case. *IEEE/ACM Transactions on Networking*, 1(3):344–357, 1993.

13. J. Regehr and J. Stankovic. HLS: A framework for composing soft real-time schedulers. In *Proc. of IEEE Real-Time Systems Symposium*, pages 3–14, December 2001.

14. S. Saewong, R. Rajkumar, J.P. Lehoczky, and M.H. Klein. Analysis of hierarchical fixed-priority scheduling. In *Proc. of Euromicro Conference on Real-Time Systems*, June 2002.

15. I. Shin and I. Lee. Periodic resource model for compositional real-time guarantees. In *Proc. of IEEE Real-Time Systems Symposium*, pages 2–13, December 2003.

Validation of Component and Service Federations in Automotive Software Applications

Luciano Baresi and Carlo Ghezzi

Dipartimento di Elettronica e Informazione - Politecnico di Milano
Piazza L. da Vinci 32, I-20133 Milano, Italy
{baresi, ghezzi}@elet.polimi.it

Abstract. The automotive domain is one of the most promising areas for component and service technologies in the near future. Vehicles are increasingly becoming integrated systems where both intra-vehicle and inter-vehicles interactions require that a set of federated components (services) be properly orchestrated. The interactions and cooperations among the members of such federations suggest the use of well-known architectural styles to properly design new systems. Among the various styles, we explore the use of the publish-subscribe paradigm for intra-vehicle cooperations and the service-oriented paradigm for vehicle-to-vehicle and vehicle-to-environment interactions. We argue that available modeling notations provide adequate support to specification, but still lack proper support to the validation phase.

In this paper we discuss component models and their validation in the context of the automotive domain. In particular, we show how publish/subscribe and service-oriented applications can be analyzed through model-checking techniques by drawing simple examples from the automotive domain.

1 Introduction

It has been argued that the automotive domain is one of the areas where component and service technologies will have the strongest impact in the near future [17]. Software, communications, and electronics are the key enabling technologies: Vehicles are increasingly becoming integrated (and intertwined) systems where network technologies enable orchestration of software components and services to provide advanced functionalities. Moreover, improvement is not only restricted to empowering advanced features within the car, but also among cars and between cars and the outside environment. Vehicles may be viewed as carriers of services, e.g., providing information on the traffic encountered during their journey, which might be shared with other vehicles. Vehicles may interact with the environment, which may provide location-aware services to the people in the vehicle.

Both intra-vehicle and inter-vehicles interactions require that a set of federated components (services) be properly orchestrated. If we think of a single vehicle, wheels and brakes, the injection control, the ABS system, but also the climate control, the Hi-Fi system, maybe the GPS receiver, and several other accessories are the to-be-coordinated components. Some of them are mandatory, but several others depend on the chosen configuration and can be added later. The interaction policies are fixed, but the overall

M. Broy, I.H. Krüger, and M. Meisinger (Eds.): ASWSD 2004, LNCS 4147, pp. 57–73, 2006.
© Springer-Verlag Berlin Heidelberg 2006

organization must consider that some components might be initially absent and join the federation dynamically.

If we think of vehicle-to-vehicle and vehicle-to-environment interactions, we can view the different vehicles (and the environment) as components that supply and require services, where the actors of a given interaction, that is, the members of the federation, cannot be fixed a-priori. It is not only a problem of understanding who is "alive" out of a predefined set (i.e., the mandatory elements and additional components that can be operated on a vehicle): available services must be discovered, negotiated, and bound dynamically.

The interactions and cooperations among the members of such federations suggest the use of well-known *architectural styles* to properly orchestrate the components. Among the many styles, we suggest two specific approaches. The *publish-subscribe* approach [21] matches quite naturally the requirements of intra-vehicle composition and coordination. The *service-oriented* paradigm [6] is particularly appealing when we move to vehicle-to-vehicle and vehicle-to-environment interactions. The use of the two different styles in the two different cases is of course not exclusive. We are making this distinction mainly to exemplify the use of the different styles in the different domains. Both component models support the required flexibility and self-configuration. Most intra-vehicle interactions do not need discovery and negotiation among components, while the changing context that underlies inter-vehicle interactions imposes them. These styles facilitate and help standardize the design phase, but how can designers reason about such federations? How do they validate designs prior to moving to the implementation phase?

Both component models have problems that make validation hard to achieve. For example, the actual communication paths of publish/subscribe models do not emerge from the design of each component in isolation, but should nevertheless be analyzed to ensure the correct behavior of the overall system. Similarly, we may think of static ways of assessing their correct match in a closed environment, but suitable run-time checking is also needed if we move to open systems. Although we argue that available modeling notations, like plain finite state machines, statecharts, UML, and automotiveUML [1], provide sufficient expressive power to specify such systems, a proper support to the validation phase is still missing. To address this problem, in this paper we tailor our research on validating software architectures ([26,5]) to the needs of the automotive domain.

Our current research efforts are mostly devoted to static analysis of architectural specifications. We investigated the validation of publish/subscribe architectures, where application-specific components are modeled using statecharts. Components interact through a special-purpose component (the *dispatcher*) that is supplied as a predefined parametric element of the specification environment. The user only needs to provide values for the parameters to tailor the behavior of the desired dispatcher, which is supplied by the adopted middleware technology.

Besides studying the interactions among components in a fixed setting, we also need to study how the topology of the system can change. This is interesting for publish/subscribe systems to understand if certain desirable properties are preserved when a component joins or leaves the federation. But it is even more interesting when we think of service-oriented architectures. In this case bindings are set at run-time and thus we need to explicitly model how they can be established. To this end, we are currently investigating the use of a *graph transformation system*, along with a *type graph* or *metamodel*, to operationally specify the dynamic semantics ascribed to the component model. It is a promising means to reason on dynamic evolutions, reconfiguration capabilities, and negotiation features.

In both cases, the analysis phase exploits model checking techniques to validate the federations of components against particular scenarios that define snapshots of the desirable global behavior of the system. Analysis techniques are exemplified on simple case studies, hopefully "realistic" in the automotive domain. Chosen examples do not aim at stressing the problem domain, rather they want to explain and demonstrate the analysis methods and motivate their application in the field.

Both analysis techniques are based on model checking techniques, which apply to finite state domains. This means that proposed methods are able to address some categories of problems, but they cannot be applied when embedded systems must be modeled as hybrid systems.

This paper is organized as follows. Section 2 introduces component models, describes the paradigms that we propose for automotive applications, and sketches a couple of simple case studies. Sections 3 and 4 present our solutions to validating interacting components. Section 5 briefly surveys related work and Section 6 concludes the paper.

2   Component Models

A component model (architectural style) defines the basic mechanisms that allow components to interact and coordinate their individual behaviors, provide some desired global behavior, and achieve some overall goals. The model defines the way individual components and services can be federated to achieve the desired global results. In the automotive domain, component models should yield fully decentralized architectures, where individual components are highly autonomous.

We see two dominant approaches to emerge in this application area: publish-subscribe and service-oriented. In the *publish/subscribe* approach (Figure 1) components do not communicate directly, but rather communication is mediated by a *dispatcher*. Components define active agents, corresponding to sensors and autonomous devices, which send events to the dispatcher (*publish*) and decide the events they want to listen to (*subscribe/unsubscribe*). The dispatcher forwards (*notifies*) events to all registered components, which react to them.

This component model easily accommodates the idea that in-vehicle services can be statically deployed out of a catalogue of options. Services may also be added and removed later on, if the need arises. Vehicle models are application families where vehicles share the same software architecture, but the set of on-board components can vary. Components can join and leave the federation in a seamless way provided that the catalogue of events, which defines the component coordination protocol, is carefully defined in advance. The global properties that define the federation are not achieved by hard-wiring the composition, but rather by agreeing on such a protocol. Since compo-

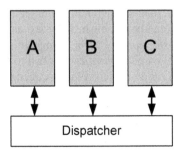

Fig. 1. Publish/subscribe systems

nents do not know the identity of each other, at any time a new component, which can react to certain events or generate other events, may be added to the system.

For example, let us refer to a HVAC (Heating Ventilation Air Conditioning) system, which regulates the temperature in the passenger compartment. Depending on the different versions of the vehicle, the system may control the compartment as a single zone or as a composition of two/three zones. The events generated by the HMI (Human Machine Interface) in the compartment are standard[1], but the way they are propagated to the heating and cooling components associated with the different zones depends on the specific configuration. Similarly, we might also envisage the case in which users want to add a new DVD player to the infotainment system of their vehicles. The HMI on board, along with the other components, should be able to interact with the newly added player without requiring that the whole software architecture be redesigned and redeployed. This is why we argue that a publish/subscribe organization may facilitate the management of different configurations.

The *service-oriented* model [6] is particularly appealing when we move to vehicle-to-vehicle and vehicle-to-environment interactions. In this case, active components, specified by a workflow, activate nonlocal services that are provided and maintained by independent authorities: for example, other vehicles or external sources which belong to the current external environment. The interaction paradigm is based on dynamic discovery of existing services and match making between a service request and a service provision, and on-the-fly composition.

Service-oriented architectures (Figure 2) involve three different kinds of logical actors: *service providers, service requesters* and *discovery agencies*. The *service provider* exposes some software functionality as a service to its clients. Such a service could, e.g., be a Web service or a Java JINI component. In order to allow clients to access the service, the provider also has to publish a description of the service. Service providers and *service requesters* usually do not know each other in advance, thus service descriptions are published via specialized *discovery agencies*, which can categorize the descriptions and provide them in response to queries issued by service requesters. As the agency returns a suitable description, which matches its requirements, the requester can start interacting with the provider and thus use the service directly.

---

[1] For the sake of simplicity, compartment zones cannot be controlled independently.

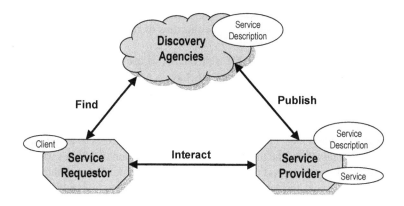

Fig. 2. Service-oriented systems

If several matches are possible, some notion of *quality of service* (such as requested accuracy, cost, trustworthiness [16]) may be used to establish the match. If none is possible, it might still be feasible to offer a degraded service based on some notion of partial match. Different *binding schemes* may thus be chosen either explicitly by the designer or as the result of negotiations – with respect to both supplied functionality and quality of service – done by the underlying runtime support (provided by the middleware). The latter notion of a highly dynamic binding supports the provision of location-aware services, by associating a service request with the specific service provider that matches the request based on the current position (context) of the car.

For example, a vehicle could inquire a map service to get the best or the cheapest map of the area. It could also access a service to compute the best itinerary to reach the final destination. The computation is not only based on static information, like the cheapest route (i.e., no fees) or the fastest one (i.e., always on highways), but also uses actual traffic conditions to better plan the itinerary. After choosing the route, the vehicle automatically pays for the fees of used highways by means of a secure external payment system.

To support these needs for a highly dynamic and evolvable architecture, we also envision situations where it should be possible to specify dynamic binding strategies not only between a service requester and a provider, but also between a service and its implementation, and between a service and its persistent data. As an example of the last point, consider the service about "traffic information on highway Paradise", initially provided by a component that is locally installed on the vehicle which delivers information based on data that are dispatched daily by the city and automatically downloaded. To get more accurate and current information, the persistent data might be automatically rebound to those acquired by a vehicle coming from that direction.

3   Interactions Among Components

Our approach to validating federations of components interacting through the publish/subscribe paradigm requires that all application-specific elements be modeled as statecharts. In contrast, the dispatcher is supplied as a pre-defined parametric component that can be tailored to capture the peculiarities of the different publish/subscribe middleware platforms.

Components are represented by UML statecharts, whose transitions describe how the component reacts to incoming events. Events have a name and a (possibly empty) set of parameters. When components subscribe/unsubscribe to/from events, they can either refer to specific events or use wildcards to address classes of events. For example, *subscribe("climate", "hot")* means that the component wants only to know when *climate* becomes *hot*, but *subscribe("climate", $)* means that it subscribes to all *climate* events.

Transitions are labelled: The first part (i.e., the precondition) describes when the transition can fire[2], while the second part defines the actions associated with the firing of the transition. For instance, the label: *consume("climate","warm") / publish("climate", "warming")* states that the transition can fire when the component is notified that someone has asked for a warmer temperature and as it fires it publishes an event to signal that the climate is warming.

The events notified to a component are stored in its notification queue. The component retrieves the first event from its notification queue and if it does not trigger any transition exiting the current state (that is, no consume operation "uses" the event), the component discards it and processes the next one. This mechanism allows components to evolve even if they receive events that cannot be processed in their current states.

For example, Figure 3 shows the statechart for a simplified *HVAC* control introduced in Section 2. For simplicity, we model the controlled temperature with two values: cold and hot. A finer granularity would simply make the example more complex.

The initial state is *Cold*. When *climate control* receives an event that asks for increasing the temperature, it moves to state *Warming* where the passenger compartment – and maybe the seats, and rearview mirrors – are warming up. As the temperature in the passenger compartment reaches a certain level, it publishes an event *hot*, which causes *climate control* to move to state *Hot*. If *HVAC* receives an event that asks for cooling the temperature inside the vehicle, its behavior is similar to the previous one and moves the control from *Hot* to *Cold*. Notice that this component ignores which other components belong to the complete configuration and interacts with them indirectly by producing events notified to all components registered to receive them. Similarly, seats and rearview mirrors subscribe to the events generated to warm the vehicle, but are not interested in those produced to cool it down.

The parametric model of the dispatcher only describes how it interacts with the other components. Currently, the dispatcher is parametric with respect to three dimensions: subscription, delivery, and notification. A *subscription parameter* specifies whether the dispatcher reacts immediately to (un)subscriptions or delays these operations. A *delivery parameter* either specifies that all events are actually delivered or that some events may be lost. Finally, a *notification parameter* specifies one of the following alternatives: the order of publication is the same as the order of notification, the order of publication and notification are the same only for the events published by the same component, or there is no relationship and events may be notified randomly.

---

[2] In this case, we only consider events and omit conditions, which would not affect the approach.

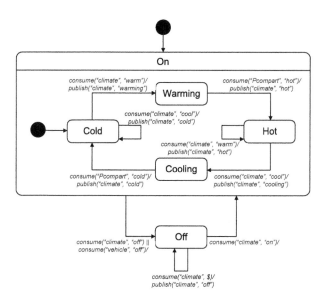

Fig. 3. Climate control

The actual dispatcher is instantiated by choosing one option for these three parameters, which cover the basic alternative the guarantees a dispatcher should satisfy. If this is not the case, developers can always override the predefined parametric component, which implements ready-to-use simple strategies, elaborate their particular model of the dispatcher as a statechart, like the other components, and integrate it in the architecture. They would loose the advantages associated with reuse and well-defined communication protocols, but the validation approach would remain the same.

After setting the model of the application, we state the properties that we want to prove. We use *Live Sequence Charts* (LSCs) [9] to describe how entities cooperate. LSCs have been selected because of their capability of representing complex scenarios that embed alternatives, parallelism, and loops[3]. Briefly, an LSC diagram describes a scenario of how the architecture behaves. Entities are drawn as white rectangles with names above. The life-cycle of an entity is rendered as a vertical line; a white rectangle indicates that the entity is created and a black rectangle indicates its death. Messages exchanged between entities are drawn as arrows and are asynchronous by default. Each message is decorated with a label that describes it.

Since the publish/subscribe paradigm defines the underlying communication policy, we omit representing the dispatcher in the charts. Each message (i.e., arrow) is first sent to the dispatcher and then routed to the other entity.

LSCs distinguish between *provisional* (or *cold*) scenarios, depicted as dashed rectangles, and *mandatory* (or *hot*) scenarios, depicted as solid rectangles, to render existential and universal properties, respectively. The former specify scenarios that must be verified in at least one evolution of the federation, while the latter identify scenarios that must hold true for all evolutions. Moreover, LSCs support the definition of *pre-conditions*

---

[3] The new UML 2 sequence diagrams offer similar modeling features.

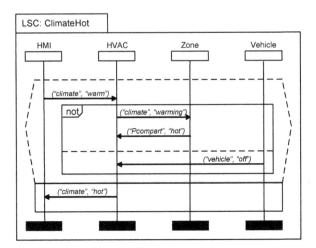

Fig. 4. An example LSC

associated with scenarios. They constrain the property (scenario) to hold only for all the evolutions in which the precondition holds true. Preconditions are drawn in dashed polygons. Within a scenario, we can describe parallel behaviors, through the *par* operator, which makes the sub-scenarios evolve in parallel without any particular order among the events they contain, and negative conditions through the *not* operator. This last operator, which is not part of standard LSCs, has two sub-scenarios as parameters and states that the first occurs only if the second does not terminate[4].

For example, the hot scenario of Figure 4 describes how to control the temperature in the vehicle. It assumes that the vehicle is subdivided in a single compartment zone. It shows the case in which the user, through the *HMI*, wants to warm up the vehicle and sends event *("climate", "warm")* to the *HVAC*. It starts by warming the *Zone*, that is, it sends event *("climate", "warming")* and then waits for the notification (event *("zone", "hot")*) from the *Zone*. The user receives event *("climate", "hot")* only if the vehicle is not switched-off in the meanwhile, that is *Vehicle* does not produce event *("vehicle", "off")*.

If the vehicle had different zones, the scenario would be more complex. The different *zones* would receive event *("climate", "warming")* in parallel. After receiving event *("zone", "hot")* from the different zones, *HVAC* generates event *("climate", "hot")* to stop the different heating systems, and also to notify the *HMI*. As before, in the meanwhile the *Vehicle* should not produce event *("vehicle", "off")*.

So far, we have shown informally how to model the federation of components and define the properties. Let us now discuss how to perform the analysis. We use the SPIN model checker [14] as verifier: everything is transformed into automata and then translated into Promela, the language to specify SPIN models. Model checking techniques have the well-known problem of state explosion, that is, the number of different states

---

[4] Notice that if scenarios only contain one message, this means that they cannot happen simultaneously.

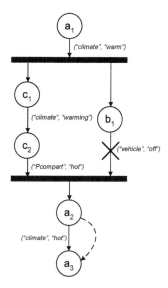

Fig. 5. The automaton that corresponds to the LSC of Figure 4

required to describe a problem may easily become unmanageable. A wise design of analysis models, along with special-purpose techniques (e.g., abstraction and bisimulation), must be adopted to mitigate the problem.

After tailoring the dispatcher according to the parameters set by the developer, we automatically generate its corresponding Promela code. The translation of statechart diagrams, for the various components, into Promela is straightforward. We do not describe this translation since it has been done by others before (e.g., vUML [20] and veriUML [7]) and we have borrowed their solutions to implement our translation.

Properties are not encoded as LTL formulae, which would be quite natural with SPIN, but are translated into automata. Since LTL does not allow the verification of existential properties (i.e., cold scenarios) natively, our solution bypasses this limitation, and also speeds up the validation process.

Validation distinguishes between existential properties (cold scenarios) and universal properties (hot scenarios). The former are tackled by predicating directly on the reachability of the final states of the automata that render the properties. The latter are addressed by means of special-purpose LTL formulae, added to the aforementioned reachability problems, to state that the hot part of the scenario must be verified for all the possible evolutions of the system. Since the general transformation process is complex, here we introduce it through an example and we invite readers to refer to [26] for a more complete presentation. The automaton of Figure 5 corresponds to the LSC of Figure 4 and has the same structure. Readers can interpret it as a statechart extended with inhibitor arcs (i.e., negative conditions). The diagram contains two parallel threads: one flow identifies the "positive" part of the *not* statement, while the other flow states the negative condition. Solid arrows describe *standard* transitions and are decorated with labels that describe recognized events[5]. Solid arrows with a cross correspond to nega-

---

[5] For the sake of simplicity, we do not describe who publishes or consumes events.

tive conditions and their firings "disable" the sub-diagrams in which they end. Dashed arrows do not define transitions between states, but constrain the evolution by means of an LTL formula: If the automaton reaches the source state of the arrow, it must always reach the target state.

In the automaton of Figure 5, the notification of the first event *("climate", "warm")* enables the fork bar that corresponds to the *not* construct of Figure 4. The automaton splits its evolution in two threads. The first thread corresponds to the warming of the passenger compartment, while the second thread corresponds to switching off the vehicle. If the first thread evolves completely while the second thread does not, the join bar is enabled and the automaton evolves to state a_2. This means that we do not switch off the vehicle while warming it. Then, the automaton reaches state a_3 with the last event (i.e., *("climate", "hot")*). By reasoning on state reachability, we can argue that, if state a_3 is reachable, the cold (simplified) version of the scenario is verified, that is, there is at least one evolution that complies with it. Since we do not want just one evolution, but we would like to prove the scenario for all evolutions, we must refine the automaton and add the dashed edge that corresponds to the LTL formula:

$$\Box(In(a_2) \Rightarrow \Diamond In(a_3))$$

to enforce the "universality" of the property. In this example, the hot scenario only comprises states a_2 and a_3 since it only has a single message ((*"climate", "hot"*)). All previous states define the precondition associated with the scenario, that is, the dashed polygon of Figure 4. The LTL formula states that, if the precondition holds (i.e., we reach state a_2), then the event must always occur and we must always end in state a_3.

We can verify this property by reasoning on state reachability. In particular, we require that the final state a_3 be reachable, thus there is at least an evolution that complies with this property. If the model checker does not highlight any evolution in which the LTL formula is violated, we can say that when the precondition is verified, the scenario is verified as well.

4   Dynamic Evolution

The validation method presented in the previous section allows designers to probe how components interact. We have shown how we exploit the peculiarities of publish/subscribe architectures to ease the modeling phase. A similar philosophy would allow other interaction paradigms to be analyzed. The drawback of the approach is that it does not support the study of how the architecture evolves during its lifetime. This is why we decided to investigate a different approach to study how federations of components can evolve dynamically. We envisage the two approaches —the one presented in this section and the other described in the previous section— to become part of an "integrated" methodology for modeling and validating software architectures, although the full integration of the two approaches is still part of our future work.

To model the dynamic changes, we describe architectural styles by means of static and dynamic models. The static part specifies components and connectors and constrains the relationships among these elements. The dynamic part defines how architectures can evolve.

We use class diagrams to model the static parts. If we think of the service-oriented paradigm, classes can be used to represent three different types of elements: *structural elements*, which specify components and services, *specification documents*, which describe services and requirements, and *messages*, which model the communication among components (services). The whole specification, presented in [5], comprises three packages Structure, Specification, and Messages which group the classes that describe the different types of elements. Here, we only present package Structure [6], Figure 6, which contains the classes that form the core of the service-oriented approach.

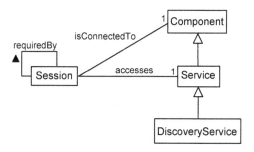

Fig. 6. Package for structural elements

Service is a special-purpose Component that exposes its features to other components and services. Sessions connect Components to Services and store the current state of the interaction between the service requester and the service. Since Service is a subclass of Component, a Service can also connect to another Service via a Session. Discovery agencies provide DiscoveryServices that are special services for querying a service catalog.

The dynamic part is specified through graph transformation rules [3] that capture the dynamic changes allowed by the architectural style. Rules are represented as a pair of collaboration diagrams. The left-hand side graph defines the pre-condition that must hold true to apply the rule, that is, the graph that must exist to enable the rule. The right-hand side graph defines the post-condition, that is, the resulting graph after applying the rule. For example, Figure 7 shows rule sendConnectRequest where a Component, which acts as service requestor, sends a request for connection to the Service it would like to connect to. The pre-condition states that the requestor must know a ServiceSpecification that couldSatisfy its Requirements. The post-condition states that the request message (ConnectRequest) is created and linked to the receiver. The elements with the same name in the left- and right-hand sides are preserved while applying the rule.

Because of space limitations, we omit the other rules, but the whole dynamic model comprises some 20 transformation rules to publish service descriptions, discover services, query the service catalog, connect to known services, interact with services, and disconnect from existing sessions. Interested readers can refer to [4] for the whole set of rules.

---

[6] No explicit cardinality means 0..n by default.

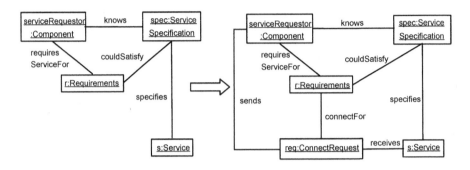

Fig. 7. Rule sendConnectRequest

Such a definition of the architectural style can be used to design consistent service-oriented systems and validate them against properties (i.e., scenarios) defined using simple sequence diagrams. In the first case, designers can define the initial configurations of their systems, and assess the compliance with the architectural style by exploiting the static part of the architectural definition. In the second case, the dynamic part of the style help reason on possible evolutions and reconfigurations and check if they are reachable given an initial configuration. In this case, the messages exchanged between components do not simply publish and notify events, but they trigger the execution of transformation rules and thus modify the topology of the architecture.

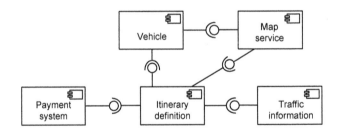

Fig. 8. A set of services for Select Itinerary

For example, let us recall the simple scenario of Section 2, and assume the availability of the set of services illustrated in Figure 8, which interact to let the Vehicle select the best itinerary and pay for the fees of the highways it uses. This component diagram defines the initial configuration from which one could start analyzing the system. Figure 9 shows an excerpt of such a model, where, for the sake of simplicity, the integrated application is rendered with a single component, which accesses the *UDDI repository* to discover services. Each provider publishes a Service specification to characterize what it offers. Details about specific parameters are hidden to keep the presented model as simple as possible. Services are linked together by means of Requirements objects, which mimic the connections of Figure 2. As already said, this model complies with the static part of the style definition (e.g., the fragment of Figure 6).

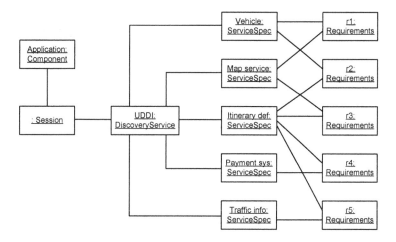

Fig. 9. A fragment of the representation of the architecture of **Select Itinerary**

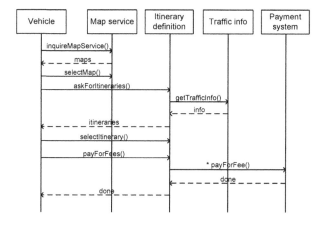

Fig. 10. A simple scenario

Designed architectures (also referred to as *configurations*) are validated against scenarios. For example, Figure 10 describes a possible interaction among the services of Figure 2, where the Vehicle (i.e., the driver) asks the Map service for the map of the area and chooses the best one. After selecting the map, it also selects the itinerary to reach its final destination. It queries Itinerary definition, which in turn queries the Traffic information service to dynamically select the best offer. Vehicle decides about the itinerary and pays for the fees of the highways it uses through Itinerary definition and the Payment system.

The scenario may embed some further requirements: (1) The vehicle asks for the cheapest map. (2) It also wants the fastest or cheapest itinerary. (3) The itinerary definition service accesses traffic information at a given frequency. (4) The vehicle uses a secure application to pay for the highway fees. To meet these requirements, in many cases, the actual services must be discovered at run-time. The actual links among the objects of the federation change while the scenario evolves and these changes are governed by transformation rules (i.e., the dynamic part of the style). This means that the analysis must state if defined rules are able to transform a given configuration of the system into another configuration that meets the new requirements. Notice that since transformation rules comply with the type graph, also the new configuration complies with the architectural style by construction.

The model checker is used to prove if there is a least a sequence of transformation rules that modifies the initial configuration as stated by the scenario. The analysis approach transforms the class diagram, graph transformation rules, and initial configuration into a Promela model by following the guidelines proposed by Varrò in [24] to feed the SPIN model-checker. It also transforms a scenario into a set of reachability properties. We check the reachability of consecutive configurations obtained from the sequence diagrams by horizontal cuts where each message (along with returned answer) is a cut. For example, if we start from the initial configuration of Figure 9, and we consider the first slice (i.e., message `inquireMapService`), the model checker has to find a sequence of rules (or single rule) to make component `Vehicle` connect to `Map service` and issue a request for a map. The rest of the scenario can be verified by a kind of assume-guarantee reasoning to reduce the computational complexity of individual verification steps. The whole process can be summarized as follows:

1. We identify relevant intermediate configurations by slicing the sequence diagram;
2. We prove that the target configuration defined by the first cut is reachable from the initial configuration;
3. If the system is in the configuration reached at the first cut, we prove that the configuration at the second cut is reachable (and this is repeated for all cuts).

Notice that since a successful proof of a reachability property does not require the traversal of the entire state space, the practical limitations of a model checking approach are not as severe as in case of safety properties, for instance.

In general, the state space constructed by the approach comprises instances for components and services, but we only consider "dynamic" elements to reduce its size. We say that an element is dynamic if there is at least one rule that potentially modifies (creates, destroys, updates) it. Since we only consider dynamic elements, the guards of the transformation rules are reduced to only check for the existence of dynamic elements.

Moreover, for model checking purposes, we must restrict the problem to be finite in size. For the graph transformation system, this restriction implies that there exists an *a priori* upper bound for the number of objects in the model for each class. Thus, we suppose that when a new object is created it is actually activated from the bounded "pool" of currently passive objects; similarly, deletion means passivation.

Graph transformation rules only consider the mechanisms that belong to the style; they ignore those details that come from the internals of services and the contents of messages. For example, they do not consider constraints associated with parameters and other restrictions imposed by the internals of services. To this end, we can complement the model checking-based analysis with simulation for more detailed results. Tools like Fujaba [10] support these in-depth validations.

5 Related Work

Given the two main directions of our research on validating software architectures, we should mention a long list of related approaches. Here, we only concentrate on the most important ones, because they inspired our solutions and are close to what we are doing.

One of the main considerations that motivated our work is that in many cases there is a mismatch between the abstraction level at which we usually model our systems and the functionality offered by current validation technologies (e.g., a UML model vs. a Promela specification). For example, this happens for vUML [20], veriUML [7], JACK [11], and HUGO [22]. They all support the validation of distributed systems through model-checking techniques. Components are specified using statecharts, but properties must be encoded using conventional temporal logics, like CTL, ACTL, and LTL.

Krüger et al. [18] use a modified version of MSCs (Message Sequence Charts) to model the cooperations among services (possible scenarios), while Inverardi et al. [15] use MSCs to specify the properties against which systems should be validated. Garlan et al. [8] and the researchers involved in the Cadena project [12] applied model-checking techniques to publish/subscribe systems. Although the goal in these two proposals is similar to ours, there are some differences: (a) our components are specified using standard UML, instead of special-purpose languages (b) our parametric dispatcher covers a wider range of behaviors, and (c) LSCs provide the operators for describing the communication among components in a natural graphical way.

As for the use of graph transformation systems to formalize the dynamics of software architectures, [19,25,23,13] used graph grammars to specify the class of admissible configurations of architectural styles. In contrast, we entrust the meta-model (i.e., the static part) with this responsibility and exploit graph transformation rules only to model dynamic aspects like evolution and reconfiguration.

6 Conclusions and Future Work

This paper has proposed an approach to specify and validate software architectures that appears to fit the requirements of an interesting class of component models in the automotive domain. A thorough assessment through case studies is needed, however, and this will be one of the challenges of future work. Other directions of future work should address the impact of encoding techniques and model-checkers on the validation process. The richness of results depends on the encoding adopted to represent artifacts in such a way that they can be used by the model checker, but it also depends on the chosen model-checker. So far we used SPIN, but we have plans to use other tools to enrich the set of considered properties. For example, we are evaluating Bogor and nuSMV to analyze different encoding techniques. We would like also to address the real-time aspects embedded in many problems in this domain. This is why we are thinking of extending our approach to make it work with timed model-checkers, like timed SPIN, Uppal and Kronos.

Our research agenda also contains the definition of proper techniques for self-healing service-oriented applications. The approaches described in this paper are applicable if the context is fixed, but service-oriented systems may be highly dynamic and the set of available services might change at run-time. This means that deployment-time analysis must be complemented with run-time monitoring, to "probe" the interactions among components, and recovery actions, to deal with anomalies. An initial outline of a possible approach has been described in [2]. More thorough experiments – also in the automotive domain – are needed to improve the approach and access its suitability.

Acknowledgments

We want to thank all the colleagues who attended the workshop for the fruitful discussions, and the anonymous reviewers for their help to ameliorate our contribution.

References

1. Automotive UML Consortium. Automotive UML Web page. www.es.tudarmstadt.de/english/research/projects/auto_uml/.
2. L. Baresi, C. Ghezzi, and S. Guinea. Towards Self-healing Compositions of Services. In *Proceedings of PRISE'04, First Conference on the PRInciples of Software Engineering*, November 2004.
3. L. Baresi and R. Heckel. Tutorial Introduction to Graph Transformation: A Software Engineering Perspective. In *Proceedings of the First International Conference on Graph Transformation (ICGT 2002)*, volume 2505 of *Lecture Notes in Computer Science*, pages 402–429. Springer-Verlag, 2002.
4. L. Baresi, R. Heckel, S. Thöne, and D. Varrò. Specification of Generic and SOA-specific Style. www.upb.de/cs/ag-engels/ag_engl/People/Thoene/MRDSA.
5. L. Baresi, R. Heckel, S. Thöne, and D. Varrò. Modeling and Validation of Service-Oriented Architectures: Application vs. Style. In *Proceedings of the European Software Engineering Conference and ACM SIGSOFT Symposium on the Foundations of Software Engineering (ESEC/FSE)*, pages 68–77. ACM press, September 2003.
6. M. Champion, C. Ferris, E. Newcomer, and D. Orchard. *Web Service Architecture, W3C Working Draft*, 2002. http://www.w3.org/TR/2002/WD-ws-arch-20021114/.
7. K. Compton, Y. Gurevich, J. Huggins, and W. Shen. An automatic verification tool for UML. Technical Report, University of Michigan, CSE-TR-423-00, 2000.
8. D. Garlan and S.Khersonsky and J.S. Kim. Model Checking Publish-Subscribe Systems. In *Proceedings of the 10th SPIN Workshop*, volume 2648 of *Lecture Notes in Computer Science*, May 2003.
9. W. Damm and D. Harel. LSCs: Breathing Life into Message Sequence Charts. *Formal Methods in System Design*, 19(1):45–80, 2001.
10. From UML to Java and Back Again: The Fujaba Web page. www.fujaba.de.
11. S. Gnesi, D. Latella, and M. Massink. Model Checking UML Statecharts Diagrams using JACK. In *Proceedings of the Fourth IEEE International Symposium on High Assuarance Systems Engineering (HASE)*, pages 46–55. IEEE Press, 1999.
12. J. Hatcliff, W. Deng, M.D. Dwyer, G. Jung, and V. Ranganath. Cadena: An Integrated Development, Analysys, and Verification Environment for Component-based Systems. In *Proceedings of the International Conference on Software Engineering (ICSE 2003)*, 2003.
13. D. Hirsch and M. Montanari. Synchronized Hyperedge Replacement with Name Mobility. In *Proceedings of CONCUR 2001*, volume 2154 of *Lecture Notes in Computer Science*, pages 121–136. Springer-Verlag, August 2001.

14. G.J. Holzmann. The Model Checker SPIN. *IEEE Transactions on Software Engineering*, 23(5):279–295, May 1997.

15. P. Inverardi, H. Muccini, and P. Pelliccione. Automated Check of Architectural Models Consistency using SPIN. In *Proceedings of the 16th IEEE International Conference on Automated Software Engineering (ASE)*, pages 349–349. IEEE Press, 2001.

16. A. Keller and H. Ludwig. The WSLA Framework: Specifying and Monitoring Service Level Agreements for Web Services. Technical Report RC22456(W0205-171), IBM Research Division, T.J. Watson Research Center, May 2002.

17. I. Krüger. Researcher in Focus. www.calit2.net/researchers/krueger/index.html.

18. I. Krüger and R. Mathew. Systematic Development and Exploration of Service-Oriented Software Architectures. In *Proceedings of the 4th Working IEEE/IFIP Conference on Software Architecture (WICSA 2004)*, pages 177–187, 2004.

19. D. Le Métayer. Software Architecture Styles as Graph Grammars. In *Proceedings of the Fourth ACM SIGSOFT Symposium on the Foundations of Software Engineering*, volume 216 of *ACM Software Engineering Notes*, pages 15–23, New York, October 16–18 1996. ACM Press.

20. J. Lilius and I.P. Paltor. vUML: a Tool for Verifying UML Models. In *Proceedings of the 14th IEEE International Conference on Automated Software Engineering (ASE)*, pages 255–258, October 1999.

21. P.A. Felber P.Th. Eugster, R. Guerraoui, and A.M. Kermarrec. The Many Faces of Publish/Subscribe. *ACM Computing Surveys*, 35(2):114/131, June 2003.

22. T. Schäfer, A. Knapp, and S. Merz. Model Checking UML State Machines and Collaborations. *Electronic Notes in Theoretical Computer Science*, 55(3):13 pages, 2001.

23. G. Taentzer, M. Goedicke, and T. Meyer. Dynamic Change Manegement by Distributed Graph Transformation: Towards Configurable Distributed Systems. In *Proceedings TAGT'98*, volume 1764 of *Lecture Notes in Computer Science*, pages 179–193. Springer-Verlag, 2000.

24. D. Varrò. Towards Automated Formal Verification of Visual Modeling Languages by Model Checking. *Journal of Software and Systems Modelling*, 2003.

25. M. Wermelinger and J. L. Fiadero. A Graph Transformation Approach to Software Architecture Reconfiguration. *Science of Computer Programming*, 44(2):133–155, 2002.

26. L. Zanolin, C. Ghezzi, and L. Baresi. An Approach to Model and Validate Publish/Subscribe Architectures. In *Proceedings of SAVCBS 2003: ESEC/FSE Workshop on Specification and Verification of Component-Based Systems*, pages 35–41, September 2003. Technical Report #03-11, Department of Computer Science, Iowa State University.

Towards a Component Architecture for Hard Real Time Control Applications

Wolfgang Pree and Josef Templ

Software Research Lab, Department of Computer Science
University of Salzburg, A-5020 Salzburg, Austria
{pree, templ}@SoftwareResearch.net

Abstract. This paper describes a new approach towards a component architecture for hard real time control applications as found, for example, in the
automotive domain. Based on the paradigm of Logical Execution Time (LET)
as introduced by Giotto [1], we adapt the high-level language construct *module*
which allows us to organize and parallelize real time code in the large. Our
module construct serves multiple purposes: (1) it introduces a namespace for
program entities and supports information hiding, (2) it represents a partitioning
of the set of actuators and control logic available in a system, (3) it acts as a
static specification of components and dependencies, (4) it may serve as the unit
of dynamic loading of system extensions and (5) it may serve as the unit of distribution of functionality over a network of electronic control units. We describe the individual usage cases of modules, introduce the syntax required to
specify our needs and discuss various implementation aspects.

1 Introduction

Hard real time control applications, as found, for example, in the automotive domain,
exhibit topologies which may be classified as (1) a single application split between
multiple computation nodes or (2) a single computation node split between multiple
applications. The latter case is considered to be of increasing importance for future
systems because of the ever increasing computation power of microcontrollers, microprocessors and the trend towards microsystems consisting of multiple logical or
physical processing units on a single chip or board. Such systems will be capable of
executing multiple control applications in parallel on a single electronic control unit
(ECU). They must, however, preserve all the timing properties of the applications as
if they were performed independently on individual ECUs. In case of the automotive
domain, the consolidation of ECUs is expected to reduce the weight and complexity
of a vehicle and to save money.

This paper describes a component architecture aiming at the goal of ECU consolidation with preservation of hard real time properties. Our approach is based on the Logical
Execution Time (LET) assumption introduced by Giotto, but expressed in a more convenient syntax (TDL = Timing Definition Language) [5], slightly changed semantics
and, most importantly, a module concept, which introduces the required abstractions for
running multiple real time control applications on a single system. Our module construct
serves multiple purposes: (1) it introduces a namespace for program entities and supports information hiding, (2) it represents a partitioning of the set of actuators and

M. Broy, I.H. Krüger, and M. Meisinger (Eds.): ASWSD 2004, LNCS 4147, pp. 74–85, 2006.
© Springer-Verlag Berlin Heidelberg 2006

control logic available in a system, (3) it acts as a static specification of components, (4) it may serve as the unit of dynamic loading of system extensions and (5) in the future it may serve as the unit of distribution of functionality across a network.

2   Key Ingredients of an Embedded Control Software Model

This section summarizes what we regard as preconditions for a solid component architecture for hard real-time applications. The concepts have been invented in the realm of the Giotto project [2] at the University of California, Berkeley.

Platform-Independent Specification of Computation and Communication Activities

Figure 1 shows a simplified, visual representation of a TDL module. A TDL module consists of a set of modes. A mode contains a set of activities, task invocations, actuator updates and mode switches. A TDL module is in one mode at a time. Mode switch conditions are checked periodically with a specified frequency. Actuactor updates are also accomplished periodically with a specified frequency.

Tasks form the units of computation. They are invoked periodically with a specified frequency. They deliver results through task output ports to actuators or to other tasks, and they read input values from sensor ports or from output ports of other tasks. Thus, a TDL model specifies the real-time interaction of a set of components with the physical world, as well as the real-time interaction between the components.

A task's functionality, that is the control laws, can be implemented in any general-purpose programming language such as C.

What makes TDL a good software model is the fact that the developer does not have to worry about platform details, for example: will the application be executed on a single node or on a distributed platform; which scheduling scheme ensures the timing behavior [4]; which device drivers copy the values from sensors or to actuators. Thus, the software model emphasizes application-centric transparency (simplicity), improves reliability and enables reuse, whereas the compiler that generates the code from the model emphasizes performance.

According to [1] a TDL program supervises the interaction between software processes and the physical world, but does not itself transform data. All computation is

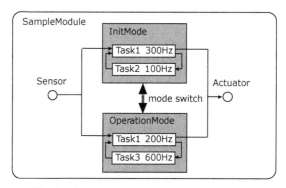

Fig. 1. Visual Representation of a TDL module

encapsulated inside the supervised software processes (tasks), which can be written in any general-purpose programming language. We refer to a TDL program as a timing program, and to the supervised processes called by the TDL program as functionality programs. A TDL program specifies only the reactivity of the functionality programs—that is, when they are invoked, and when their outputs are read—but not their scheduling.

The Logical Execution Time (LET) Assumption and Its Implications
The key property of the TDL semantics is the *Logical Execution Time* (LET) assumption, which means that the execution times associated with all computation and communication activities are fixed and determined by the model, not the platform. In TDL, the logical execution time of a task is always exactly the period of the task, and the logical execution times of all other activities (mode switching, data transfer across links, etc.) are always zero. For example, the task labelled Task1 in the Operation-Mode in Figure 1 logically executes for 5 micro seconds, which implies that (1) it reads its input at the beginning of its period, and (2) its output is not available to other tasks before 5 micro seconds, even if the actual execution of the task on the CPU finishes earlier.

According to [1] a TDL model is *environment determined*: for any given behavior of the physical world seen through the sensors, the model computes a *unique* trace of actuator values at periodic time instants. In other words, the only source of non-determinism in a TDL system is the physical environment. This makes the validation of the system considerably easier and forms the precondition for real-time compositional models. Thus, our component architecture relies on preserving the LET assumption.

3 LET-Based Components

The subsequent sections present our modular architecture for control applications that rely on the LET assumption. The corresponding language constructs are part of TDL.

Introducing Modules
As a first step towards a modular architecture for hard real time control systems, we introduce the notion of a module as a container of a Giotto program. Thus, all code belonging to a traditional Giotto application is textually enclosed inside a module. The module construct starts with the keword 'module' followed by the name of the module and a pair of curly brackets, which represent the namespace introduced by the module. The following example shows the skeleton of a module.

```
module EngineControl {

    //Giotto/TDL code consisting of sensor, actuator,
    //task and mode declarations

}
```

As a consequence, we arrive at Giotto programs as named entities, which may be handled by an appropriate runtime system on an ECU. Such a runtime system, also called an embedded machine (E-machine, see [1]), may load and execute multiple modules in parallel. It should be noted that a module must only be loaded once into an E-machine and it stays loaded until the E-machine terminates or there is some user interaction, which unloads the module explicitly. It is up to the runtime system being used on an ECU if modules can be loaded dynamically or if a static configuration has to be provided.

CPU Partitioning

A module may provide a *start* mode, which is the mode the application is executing after loading the module into an ECU. Executing a module implies the reservation of a percentage of the available CPU time for execution of this module, given that the CPU is fast enough to execute this module in addition to possibly other modules loaded before. A module which needs to reserve a percentage of the CPU is called a 'partition' and splitting the CPU between multiple partitions is called 'CPU partitioning'. A module which does not provide a start mode will not be executed, which means, it will not need a CPU partition. This can be meaningful to define a module which exports constants, types and sensors only.

Assuming that an E-machine provides the means to dynamically load a module, this can be used for handling the usage case 'dynamic partitioning'. At runtime, an arbitrary module may be loaded upon request by the user, thus leading to a set of independently loaded modules. Of course, the set of modules to be loaded into a particular E-machine may be configured in some configuration file, but this is not standardized and not known to the E-machine.

Module Import

In order to allow the decomposition of large applications into smaller parts and to allow expressing dependencies between modules statically, the module concept provides an import mechanism, which allows a client module to specify that it depends on a service module and accesses public elements of the imported module. The import relationship forms a directed acyclic graph (DAG) between client and service modules.

```
module AdvancedCar{

    import EngineControl;
    import BrakeByWire;
    import ...;

    //Giotto/TDL code consisting of sensor, actuator,
    //task and mode declarations;
    //may access public elements of imported modules
}
```

Loading a client module into an E-machine implies loading of all imported service modules unless they have been loaded before. Each of the modules may have its own start mode, thus multiple partitions may be required in order to perform loading of a client module. In this case, however, it is known statically which modules must be loaded due to the static import relationship. Thus, the usage case 'static partitioning' is dealt with by means of module imports.

While it is obvious that using imported constants, types and sensors does not pose any semantic difficulties, it is not a priori clear how to treat constructs such as tasks, modes and actuators.

Multiple modules may read the same sensors, for example, but what happens if multiple modules write to the same actuators? Note that any of the parallel running modules may be in one of several modes and it is not statically defined which actuators are under control of which module at which time. Therefore it must be prevented that multiple modules write to the same actuator. We simply restrict an actuator update to the module the actuator is declared in. Thus, the module construct acts as a partitioning of the set of actuators. In a large application, sensors could be declared in a common service module, from where they can be used in any client module. A client module declares a subset of the actuators of the complete system and provides the functionality and timing to set their values. Reading the actuator value is permissible by any client module if an actuator is made visible.

Information Hiding

According to popular programming languages we use the keyword 'public' to mark program elements as being publicly visible. There is no need (so far) for a corresponding keyword 'private', as this is the default anyway and there is no further level of visibility.

```
module EngineController {
  public const maxRpm = 6500;
  //... more code
}
```

As mentioned above, package or assembly level visibility of names is not provided by our module concept. There is, however, a simple way of mapping external functionality code to packages (Java) or name spaces (C++, C#). We allow to use structured module names, i.e. module names are allowed to contain a dot. All module name parts up to the rightmost '.' are mapped to packages in Java and namespaces in C++ or C#. Within the TDL module, structured module names are references by using the rightmost name part only. The detailed mapping rules are defined for every individual language mapping and cannot be specified in general. A mapping to ANSI C, for example, might replace the '.' by '_' in order to get unique and valid names for external functions.

Mode Extension

Mode extension is an experimental feature we are currently working on. It means to add or even override activities of a particular mode specified in a separate module. Such a feature may, for example, be useful for hot deployment of new functionality or for fixing errors of a mode without making any source code changes in the erroneous module. An extended mode inherits the mode period from its base mode.

```
module ExtendedEngineControl {
  import EngineControl;
  actuator int newActuator uses setNewActuator;
  task newTask ...; //provides output variable 'res'
  mode normal extends EngineControl.normal {
    task [1] newTask(...);
    actuator [1] newActuator := newTask.res;
  }
}
```

This example adds a task invocation and an actuator update to mode *normal* of module *EngineControl*. The extensions get into effect only when module *ExtendedEngineControl* is loaded into an E-machine.

A particular problem arises if a mode is extended multiple times. Since all activities of a mode (task invocation, actuator update, and mode switch) must be deterministic, i.e. there must for example be only one mode switch guard that evaluates to true, there must not be an arbitrary set of mode extensions available in a system. Therefore we limit mode extensions to a single extended mode, which may be extended itself by another single mode, thus leading to a sequence of extensions rather than a tree.

Scheduling Issues

In order to preserve the timing behavior of all concurrently executed applications, it is required to adapt the scheduling strategy to this requirement. We are currently experimenting with a simple time sharing strategy based on preemptive scheduling. The basic idea is as follows.

As introduced above a partition corresponds to a module with a start mode. The greatest common divisor of all activity periods of all modes of all partitions must be calculated. This is called the 'partition period' and has the obvious property that no event (task invocation, actuator update, mode switch) happens during this period. The partition period defines the period of time, which will be shared by all partitions according to their needs. A CPU intensive partition will get a higher percentage of the partition period than a less CPU intensive partition. The percentage needed for a partition is determined by the most CPU intensive mode of the partition and may be regarded as a fixed slot inside the partition period. Within the slot of the partition period assigned to a particular partition, this partition may perform any calculations and it may execute in any mode. Due to the calculated size of the slot, there is litte waste of CPU time. When all partitions execute their most CPU intensive mode, the CPU will be allocated up to 100%.

When loading and scheduling a new partition, it must be checked if the former partition period needs to be changed because of the activity periods of the new partition will not be a multiple of the old partition period. If there is a change, all partitions must be rescheduled for the new partition period, otherwise it suffices to schedule the new partition only and check if there is a slot within the partition period available for it which is large enough to execute the most CPU intensive mode of the new partition.

In practice, there are only a few periods commonly in use (e.g. 500, 1000, 10000 usecs) and these tend not to be prime numbers. In case of primes, the partition period would get as small as 1 time unit, which is 1 microsecond in our implementation. This would produce large scheduling tables and would not allow splitting the partition period into several slots.

(Re-)Scheduling can be done in the background in parallel to the execution of real-time applications: The scheduling algorithm is executed in a thread which runs whenever the ECU would be idle anyway. In other words, coming up with a possibly new schedule is not constrained by a real-time deadline. Only after finishing the scheduling (or rescheduling) there may be an update of the runtime data structures, but this is a very simple step which can be regarded as executing in logical zero time.

Example TDL Modules

The following TDL source code shows two modules M1 and M2. M1 exports three named constants and two tasks, and M2 imports M1 and may therefore access the exported entities. Module M1 defines two modes of operation, f11 and f12, where f11 is the start mode. Both modes invoke two tasks inc and dec and check the mode switch condition once per mode period, which in both cases is 10ms. The difference between the two modes is that in f12 the task dec will be invoked twice as fast as in f11. Module M2 defines a single mode, which uses the outputs of tasks inc and dec in order to calculate the sum and update an actuator. Depending on the mode of M1, the output will be a constant value or it will change over time. As a developer specifies only the timing behavior in TDL, the functionality of the tasks has to be implemented in another programming language. The functions invoked by the tasks, the drivers for reading sensors and updating actuators, and the guards for conditional execution can be implemented in any general-purpose programming language such as C. The external functionality code is indicated by the keywords uses and if.

```
module M1 {

  public const
    c1 = 50; c2 = 200; refPeriod = 10ms;

  sensor
    int s uses getS;

  public task inc {    // wcet=1ms
    output int o := c1;
    uses incImpl(o);  // inc. by step 10
  }

  public task dec {    // wcet=1ms
    output int o := c2;
    uses decImpl(o);  // dec. by step 10
  }

  start mode f11 [period=refPeriod] {
    task
      [freq=1] inc(); // LET of task inc is 10/1 = 10ms
      [freq=1] dec();
    mode
      [freq=1] if switch2m2(s, inc.o) then f12;
  }

  mode f12 [period=refPeriod] {
    task
      [freq=1] inc();
      [freq=2] dec();  // LET of task dec is 10/2 = 5ms
    mode
      [freq=1] if switch2m1(s, inc.o) then f11;
  }
}
```

```
module M2 {

  import M1;

  actuator
    int a := M1.c2 uses setA;

  public task sum {  // wcet=1ms
    input int i1; int i2;
    output int o := M1.c2;
    uses sumImpl(i1, i2, o);
  }

  start mode main [period=M1.refPeriod] {
    task
      [freq=1] sum(M1.inc.o, M1.dec.o);
    actuator
      [freq=1] a := sum.o;
  }
}
```

Figure 2 shows the outputs of module M1's inc and dec tasks, and module M2's sum task. Module M1 is in mode f11 at the beginning, therefore the sum task is producing a constant output. After pushing the sensor button, a mode switch occurs and task sum produces the corresponding output pattern. The delay between the output of the sum task and the output of the inc and dec tasks is due to the LET semantics.

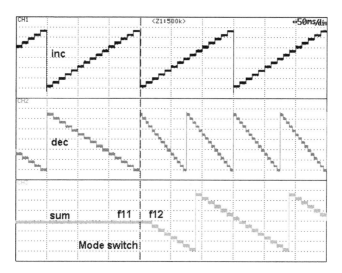

Fig. 2. Functional and temporal behavior of modules M1 (mode f11 and then f22) and M2

Implementation Status

We have implemented a variant of Giotto called TDL by using the compiler generator tool Coco [6]. An experimental runtime system based on Java threads, which are not strictly real time but serve well as a test bed for our architecture, has been implemented. Execution of parallel partitions is possible and scheduling works as described above. In addition we are working on an implementation of our architecture based on industry standard operating systems such as OSEK and OSEK/Time to get a detailed knowledge about what is really possible under these platforms and what is not. We are currently considering to port our Java based E-machine to 'realtime' Java.

4   Distributed TDL Components—Outlook and Related Work

During the course of the development of our modular architecture for control systems, it became clear that modules may serve another purpose, namely as unit of distribution. In an analogy to general-purpose programming languages, a TDL task corresponds to a function and a TDL module corresponds to a module in languages such as Oberon or Ada. A TDL module is supposed to encapsulate the functionality that is put on one ECU in current automotive system designs, such as the all-wheel-drive control system or the engine control system. This implies that TDL modules exhibit weak dependencies on each other, corresponding to weak coupling between modules, whereas one TDL module has a narrow interface and strong cohesion. This means that TDL modules are a perfect choice as units of distribution of functionality across a network of ECUs in case that the CPU or I/O of a single node is not capable of handling all the control tasks. In the following we sketch the development scenario that illustrates how the complexity of distributed system implementation is significantly reduced compared to state-of-the-art approaches.

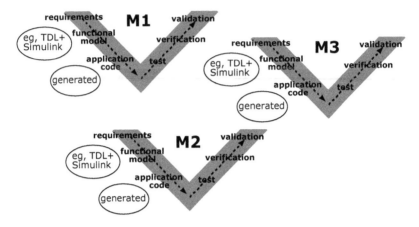

Fig. 3. V-Cluster-Life-Cycle

Application-Centric Development
The key benefit of the development methodology that results from the TDL component architecture is that a developer does not have to worry from the beginning whether the overall system is going to be executed on a single ECU or a distributed platform. The distribution of the TDL modules is either generated automatically or specified later in the development process (see below). Figure 3 shows what we call the V-Cluster-Life-Cycle: Modules are developed independently of each other. Each V-Life-Cycle delivers a TDL module. The TDL modules are separate units of compilation. The behavior (timing and functionality) of the modules is unchanged no matter how they are distributed on a specific platform. A time-safety check ensures that the timing requirements can be met.

If the modules should be executed on a distributed platform, the modules have to be assigned to ECUs on the particular platform. We might find heuristics that allow an automatic assignment of modules to ECUs. For example, one aspect that needs to be considered in the distribution is that the network traffic between the ECUs is minimized. Thus modules should be close to their sensors and actuators if possible. The idea is that a tool proposes a distribution of the modules, if one can be found that satisfies the timing requirements. The proposed distribution can then be changed manually if necessary. Basically, the distribution can be described in a table like that:

module	@
M1	ECU1
M2	ECU2
M3	ECU1

A visual/interactive editor could more conveniently support the editing of the assignments. The developer could also view the current CPU usage that would be updated according to the modules assigned to one ECU.

Model-Based Development
Besides the TDL program the developer has to come up with the functionality code. Figure 4 shows a sample model-based tool chain that assumes that Simulink is used for modeling the functionality (control laws). The Simulink simulation environment can be used to validate the behavior of the modules and their interaction before the code is generated from the models. For further details we refer to the contribution *Simulink Integration of Giotto/TDL* in this LNCS publication.

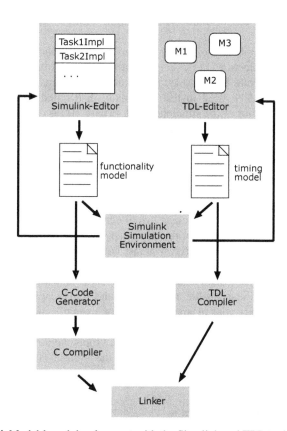

Fig. 4. Model-based development with the Simulink and TDL tool chain

Software-Bus Abstraction
Besides the TDL program and the functionality code, the developer has to come up with getter and setter functions, which copy values from the environment to sensors and from actuators back to the environment. To simplify the implementation of getter and setter functions in the realm of a distributed system, we aim at providing the abstraction of a set of globally available sensors and actuators, which we call a *software*

bus. The implementation of the software bus for common networks in the automotive domain, such as (TT-)CAN, FlexRay and the TTA, along with the distribution of modules as sketched above will be our next major steps towards a full-fledged component architecture for control applications.

Related Work

Various methods and tools aim at the development of distributed control applications. For example, DaVinci [7] and SysDesign [8] represent the state-of-the-art method and tool support. Both have in common that they help the developer to simulate the behavior of the control system(s) on a distributed platform. The important difference to the TDL component architecture is that these methods do not rely on software models so that the developer still has to perform the activities in a platform-centric manner. That is, the developer has to build the application with the selected distributed platform in mind.

Nevertheless, some of the tools could be used to simplify the implementation of the TDL component architecture. For example, DaVinci could simplify a suitable implementation of the software bus abstraction on certain platforms. This has to be evaluated. SysDesign could be used to test the finally distributed TDL modules and to validate that the behavior of the simulated TDL program(s) is equivalent to the executables. SysDesign would have to be checked whether it can indeed provide the necessary granularity for such virtual prototypes.

Several other approaches for modeling real-time properties exist. For a comparison with synchronous languages we refer to [9]. It is unclear whether it will be possible to provide efficient code generators based on the UML profile for performance, schedulability and time [10]. As this UML profile specification is work in progress it needs to be compared with TDL in the future. Architecture Description Languages (ADLs) such as Wright [11] do not consider real-time aspects. The Rapide [12] ADL relies on the event-based paradigm of reactive systems, not on the time-triggered paradigm as TDL does.

Figure 5 shows the abstraction levels of the various approaches. Besides the platform-centric approach state-of-the-art methods and tools imply a non-deterministic behavior of (composed) control applications. For example, both DaVinci and SysDesign deal with task priorities. The composition of task sets could, for example, result in race conditions. In other words, with such tools the developer has the chance to detect and fix anomalies, hopefully before the system is delivered to the real

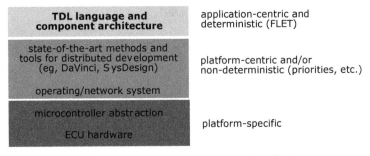

Fig. 5. Abstraction levels for control application development

platform. But the methods and tools do not provide the appropriate abstractions so that a straight-forward, error-free composition is guaranteed.

Acknowledgements

We thank Christoph Kirsch for supporting us in understanding and extending the Giotto ideas. Emilia Coste and Claudiu Farcas provided valuable feedback on the TDL compiler while they worked on a plugin for generating output for an ANSI-C based E-machine. They also helped to shape the scheduling algorithm currently in use in the Java based E-machine. Michael Holzmann, Sebastian Fischmeister, Guido Menkhaus and Gerald Stieglbauer provided valuable input during informal discussions and group meetings.

This research was supported in part by the FIT-IT Embedded Systems grant 807144 provided by the Austrian government through the Bundesminsterium für Verkehr, Innovation und Technologie.

References

1. T. Henzinger, C. Kirsch, W. Pree, M. Sanvido: From Control Models to Real-Time Code Using Giotto; IEEE Control Systems Journal, February 2003, Vol. 23 No.1, Special Issue on Software-Enabled Control
2. Web reference: http://www-cad.eecs.berkeley.edu/~fresco/giotto/
3. N. Wirth: Tasks versus threads: An alternative multiprocessing paradigm, Software-Concepts and Tools, vol. 17, pp. 6-12, 1996.
4. T.A. Henzinger: Masaccio: A formal model for embedded components, in Proc. 1st IFIP Int. Conf. Theoretical Computer Science, LNCS 1872, Springer Verlag, 2000, pp. 549-563.
5. Josef Templ. TDL Specification and Report. Technical report, Software Research Lab, University of Salzburg, Austria, October 2003. http://www.SoftwareResearch.net/site/publications/C055.pdf
6. Mössenböck, H.: Coco/R for Java.http://www.ssw.uni-linz.ac.at/Research/Projects/Coco/Java/
7. DaVinci tools: http://www.vector-informatik.de/
8. SysDesign tools: http://www.cadence.com/
9. C.M. Kirsch, 2002, Principles of Real-Time Programming. *In Proceedings of EMSOFT 2002, Grenoble* LNCS, 2491.
10. UML profile: http://www.omg.org/technology/documents/formal/schedulability.htm
11. Wright ADL: http://www.cs.cmu.edu/afs/cs/project/able/www/wright/index.html
12. Rapide ADL: http://pavg.stanford.edu/rapide/

Adding Value to Automotive Models

Eckard Böde[1], Werner Damm[1], Jarl Høyem[1],
Bernhard Josko[1], Jürgen Niehaus[2], and Marc Segelken[1]

[1] Kuratorium OFFIS e.V. Safety Critical Systems, Escherweg 2,
26121 Oldenburg, Germany
{boede, damm, hoyem, josko, segelken}@offis.de
http://www.offis.de/
[2] Carl von Ossietzky University Oldenburg
Ammerländer Heerstr. 114-118, D-26129 Oldenburg, Germany
Juergen.Niehaus@Informatik.Uni-Oldenburg.DE
http://ses.informatik.uni-oldenburg.de/

Abstract. We report on how implementing a Model Based Automotive
SW Engineering Process in an industrial setting can ensure the correctness of automotive applications when a process based on formal models
is used. We show how formal methods, in particular model checking, can
be used to ensure consistency of the models and can prove that the models satisfy selected functional and safety requirements. The technique
can also be used to automatically generate test vectors from the model.
Hence we show how in many ways formal verification techniques can add
value to the models used for different purposes in developing automotive
applications.

1 Introduction

Figure 1 taken from a public presentation[1] of Dr. Frischkorn, Head of Electronic
System Development, BMW Group, shows the exponential growth in electronic
components in cars, spanning all segments from power train, body electronics,
active and passive safety, as well as navigation and infotainment. Today, up to
40% of the total vehicle cost originate from the cost of electronic components,
with 50-70% of this share taken by embedded software development. The key
strategic role of electronic components in cars is expected to expand - 90% of all
innovations are driven by electronic components and software.

This exponential increase in functionality comes together with two other
sources of complexity: increasingly one function is shared across multiple electronic control units (ECUs), i.e. it requires the correct and timely interaction
of multiple sub-functions distributed over multiple ECUs. Such distributed hard
real-time systems contrast drastically in complexity with the typically single
ECU based technologies, for which electronic design processes in place today
where optimized, and lead directly to complex interfaces between OEMs and

---

[1] ARTIST and NSF Workshop on Automotive Software Development, San Diego,
USA, Jan 2004.

M. Broy, I.H. Krüger, and M. Meisinger (Eds.): ASWSD 2004, LNCS 4147, pp. 86–102, 2006.

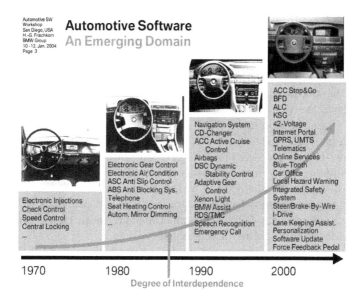

Fig. 1. Automotive Software - An Emerging Domain

multiple suppliers (in contrast to the traditional situation where one supplier used to provide a complete solution). Finally, the introduction of new technologies such as X-by-wire (e.g. "brake-by-wire", such as needed for fully automatic distance control), mandate introductions of new technologies (such as time-triggered architectures), for which there is no established design practice today.

Jointly, these drastic changes in the development of electronic automotive components have lead to an increased level of failures of electronic components, sometimes making headlines news[2]. As recently reported in "Die Welt"[3], Germany has seen 940 000 cars impacted by call-back actions. The German Automotive Club ADAC reports, that 50 % of all failures treated where due to failure in electronic components.

Multiple lines of attack have been launched by the automotive industry to counter such developments. In particular, there is an increasing trend towards so-called *model-based development*, in which the largely textual way of requirement capturing, still wide-spread today, is replaced by the creation of *executable specification models*, often referred to as *model-based development*.

---

[2] Spiegel On-Line reported in May 12, 2003, that the finance minister of Thailand was caught in his BMW due to a failure of the central locking system, further impaired by a failing climate control system. PC magazine reported in January 2001, that Ford has acknowledged a software bug in the cruise control chip, causing the car to dash backwards when entering reverse.

[3] Die Welt, 15.1.2004.

Companies have adopted various use cases to capitalize on such specification models. For OEMs, typical use cases include *virtual system integration* (allowing to simulate the distributed realization of automotive functions *prior* to contracting suppliers for the development of sub-functions), *concept validation* for individual sub-functions, assuring that the required functionality can be realized, and the use of specification models as a basis of contracts with suppliers. Typical use-cases on the supplier side include *concept validation* and *automatic code generation*, where production quality C-code is automatically generated from specification models.

Such model-based processes allow a significant improvement of design quality, but fail to address the process of quality assurance. So far classical testing was employed to ensure the correctness of the design or the implementation and although this approach also benefits from model-based processes it is far from being able to compensate for the exponential increase in complexity and the increasingly distributed nature of functionality.

Classical approaches to testing are guided by the test-engineers intuition and experience in designing "good" test cases, which have a high likelihood in exposing errors. In the ideal case, the test cases for *acceptance testing* (of ECUs delivered by the supplier) and integration testing cover all relevant behaviour based on textual requirement documents in order to expose design faults.

With today's size of ECU processing 50 to 1000 sensor and actuator signal bits, 10 to 30 internal sub-functions running in parallel, each with about 20 to 100 key states, the number of possible state combinations are reaching an order far above 50^{20} possible state combinations, a number that cannot be handled by test-engineers intuition and experience any more, not mentioning fixed-point and floating-point representations of continuous items such as brake pressure, acceleration, speed, RPMs, etc, which pushes the complexity to astronomical degrees.

It is this sheer astronomical complexity, which in quantitative terms expresses the so called *testing gap* - it is simply impossible even for the most qualified test-engineer to come up with good test cases. The challenging question is, how in this jungle can he ever hope to find those critical scenarios, which expose the designers errors - and these are bound to be there.

This paper describes three approaches addressing the testing gap, all *automating* test-generation in different, use-case specific ways. All test-automation solutions are based on techniques for automatic exploration of extremely large state-spaces, which capitalize on leading edge research results and extensive industrial experience in the usage of this technology. The approaches are

1. Formal verification technology for certification, debugging, regression verification and virtual integration check
2. Automatic generation of test vectors
3. Fault-tree analysis

The technologies have been fully integrated with a range of tools in industrial usage today for developing specification models, including ASCET-SD [1] from ETAS, Matlab-Simulink/Stateflow from The MathWorks, Statemate and

Rhapsody from I-Logix, and Scade [2] from Esterel Technologies. All tool names are trademarks of the respective companies. We will outline the ESACS project for the application of fault-tree analysis and the SafeAir project for the other formal approaches as examples of how these technologies can be used in the design process. We consider the integration of the presented methods with industry standard CASE tools to be a prerequisite for the introduction of such methods into the industrial design process for electronic control units. This paper will de-emphasize the chosen lines of attach for integration COTS development tools with the underlying mathematical algorithms - we refer the reader to papers cited above for examples of the chosen integration approaches.

2   Formal Verification Technology

Formal verification techniques are able to mathematically prove or disprove that a formally given reactive system follows certain formal requirements. During the last decade, formal verification techniques, like model checking (*cf.* [3]) or theorem proving (*cf.* PVS [4], Isabelle [5], *etc.*), have been pushed by researchers from the CAV and Hybrid Systems community (*e. g.*, [6], [7]) to increase both, the level of complexity of systems and the class of models amenable for *automatic* formal verification. Today, automatic verification techniques are further developed in a wide variety of research projects, *e. g.*, PATH[4], MoBIES[5], SafeAir[6], Omega[7], AVACS[8], and Verisoft[9], as well as being used in industrial design processes (*cf.* [8]).

   To cope with full ECU models, these techniques combine a range of analysis engines like Binary Decision Diagrams (BDDs, [9,10]), satisfiability checkers (SAT, [11,12]), constraint solvers ([13,14]), decision procedures ([15,16]), linear programming ([17]), abstraction refinement ([18,19]), predicate abstraction ([20,21]), *etc.* Current trends in development will result in a further increase of automation especially for the verification of hybrid systems ([22]) as well as a semantic integration with industry standard CASE tools to enable their integration into industrial design flows (see below).

   We are not going into details to describe these well known techniques since the focus of this paper is to present different application scenarios in which these techniques are used. The interested reader is refered to the cited literature for any details.

3   Formal Verification Application

Once the formal verification techniques mentioned in the previous section are integrated with a user-friendly easy-to-use and easy-to-understand graphical user

---

[4] see www-path.eecs.berkely.edu
[5] see www.rl.af.mil/tech/programs/MoBIES
[6] see www.safeair.org
[7] see www.omega.imag.fr
[8] see www.avacs.org
[9] see www.versoft.de

interface, also engineers without scientific background are able to apply these throughout various steps of the development process. We extend the term "formal verification" to cover the following use cases, each of them being discussed below:

- Certification of ECUs
- Formal Debugging
- Regression testing
- Compositional / Grey box testing

3.1   Use Case 1: Certification of ECU Models

Formal verification can give complete coverage of a model with respect to functional, safety and real-time requirements, i.e. certain techniques such as BDD-based symbolic modelchecking are able to mathematically prove that no reachable state of the system violates the requirement. Examples of the different types of requirements are:

- Functional requirement: "An Intrusion alarm will be activated when window is crashed."
- Safety requirement: "Steering wheel will never be locked when ignition is on."
- Real-time requirement: "Air bag fires at most 15 milliseconds after a crash."

With such certification it is possible to create "golden devices" that can be used e.g. as a supplier specification or later as a maturity gate prior to sign-off. This significantly reduces the potential for call-backs. Certification can also be used to show compliance to standards imposed by certification authorities for SIL 3,4 applications, such as Cenelec EN 50128 - B.30, DO 178B or IEC 61508.

Requirements like the previously given example ones are usually formalized with some temporal logic which can be processed directly by the formal techniques. However such logics have shown to be hard to understand and thus suffer from a low acceptance in industrial contexts. In order to improve on this acceptance criteria, a higher level mechanism is required which offers a simpler way of specifying formal requirements.

A commercially available tool offering such functionality is the ModelCertifier, a formal verification tool offering *100% coverage of specification models* in detecting potential violations of style guides or requirements being formalized with the help of a pattern library of typical temporal idioms. It includes patterns like never P, always P, P not before Q, P within t time units after Q etc, where P and Q are conditions on data items or states of the ECU. Technically ModelCertifier generates observer automata out of these temporal idioms and links them to the model behavior, very much the same as if the model itself would have been enriched by a parallel component which rises a dedicated failure signal if the property to be observed is violated. The remaining algorithm consists of an invariance check with symbolic modelchecking that analyses whether the introduced failure signal can get true. The algorithm explores *all* possible execution scenarios, taking into account *all* possible readings of interface objects, e.g. all possible CAN-bus messages, or all possible sensor readings - and this over an unbounded run-time. It attacks the testing gap by *automatically* exercising *all possible paths* through the specification model - whereas each manually specified test-case would only address a *single* path. A key enabler of industrial usage of these techniques rests in the ability to fully automate this process - this in spite of the complexity of today's electronic components.

The certification procedure on typical industrial ECU models often ranges within 30 to 300 seconds, but can take considerable more time for bigger models. However, for e.g. the formal verification of 36 requirements for an Airbag controller for a total certification the required time is 20 minutes, which is the typical amount of time needed for such ECUs.

3.2   Use Case 2: Formal Debugging

The power of detecting whether certain states in an ECU is rechable or not is not restricted to be used for certification purposes only. It is also a very powerful technique in the debugging process, called formal debugging. Instead of manually creating and running lots of simulation scenarios with the aim of analysing the latest modifications, the engineer can use automatic formal techniques instead to check e.g. if his newly introduced state is reachable, if non-determinism is still absent or if the local invariant still holds. This saves a lot of development time since the simulation scenarios do not have to be created and checked manually.

Commercially available for this use case is e.g. the Statemate ModelChecker, which can be used to check the consistency of Statemate models automatically. It is optimized for ease of use and fast turn-around times, thus aiming at supporting the typical engineer developing a particular application. It offers several analysis checks to debug specification models. It is used for formal debugging and replaces hundreds of simulation runs by one verification run. Technically it uses the same formal techniques as the ModelCertifier, BDD-based symbolic modelchecking and satisfiability of boolean formulas in combination with automatic abstraction techniques.

To give an idea on the required execution time of such checks the following list shows some state reachability verification time examples on complete ECU models averaged over all states:

- Autopilot: 30 minutes
- Central locking: 2 minutes
- EMF: 2,5 minutes
- Car-Alarm: 3 minutes
- Airbag: 1 minute

3.3   Use Case 3: Using Formal Verification for Regression Testing

The possibilities of the techniques of certification and formal debugging allow their application in a third related use case, commonly known as regression testing. In classical regression testing, the created simulation scenarios are run

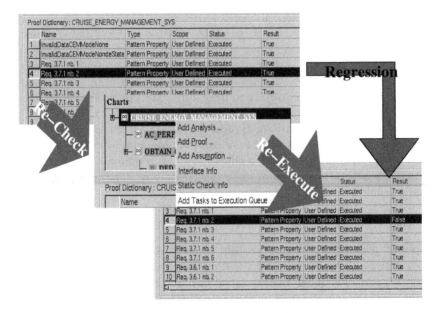

Fig. 2. Regression Testing the Model

after each change to the executable model to check if the behavior covered by these scenarios is still as expected.

However, this can only reveal faults that were covered by one of the existing scenarios and thus suffers from the inherent incompleteness of test cases for practical reasons. Here the combination of regression tests and formal techniques result in a powerful approach that would best be described by the term regression verification, although this term is not commonly used yet.

As opposed to classical regression testing, this approach again covers the whole behavior of the model for each of the previously specified certification or formal debugging test goals. Again, this exhibits any problem and not only the one an already available test scenario has been created for.

The tight integration of the formal verification tools inside the CASE tool allows an easy application of such regression verification since for a given list of proof goals a single button-press runs the whole suite, as implied in figure 2 for the already mentioned ModelChecker/ModelCertifier for Statemate.

3.4   Use Case 4: Virtual Integration Test and IP Protection

Formal verification techniques can be used to do a virtual integration test in an early design phase. On the one hand a virtual integration test highly reduces the number of errors not caught until sub-system integration test. On the other hand virtual integration test supports Intellectual Property (IP) protection of subsystems designed by third parties.

Virtual integration can technically be established by compositional reasoning [23]. The general goal of compositional reasoning is to derive a global system

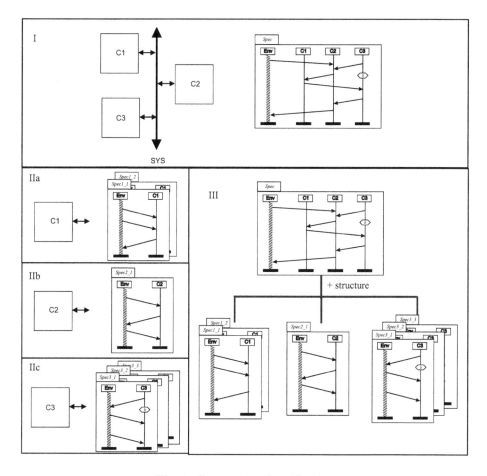

Fig. 3. Compositional verification

property from properties of its components. Figure 3 illustrates the system-level verification method based on compositional reasoning. Basic components are checked using for example ordinary model checking techniques. Composed structural units are verified by deriving the specification out of properties of its components.

A compositional verification step is based on

- a property of the composed system which should be checked,
- properties of the components, and
- structure and communication between the components.

Let us consider the example system shown in Figure 3. The goal is to verify that the global system *SYS* satisfies the property *Spec*. To derive this property several steps have to be done:

1. At component level, prove appropriate properties of the components:
   - $Spec1\_1$ and $Spec1\_2$ for component $C1$,   (IIa)
   - $Spec2\_1$ for component $C2$,   (IIb)
   - and $Spec3\_1$, $Spec3\_2$ and $Spec3\_3$ for component $C3$.   (IIc)
2. At the system level derive the global specification from the component properties:
   - $Spec$ is logically derivable from
     $Spec1\_1$, $Spec1\_2$, $Spec2\_1$, $Spec3\_1$, $Spec3\_2$ and $Spec3\_3$ together with the structure and the communication mechanism on system level.
     (III)

To do the compositional proof step (III) at system level no implementation details of the components are required. The step is based only on the formal requirement specifications of the components. Hence this approach supports IP protection in a manufacturer/suppliers design chain. The correctness of the components is guaranteed by the suppliers. A supplier can use, for example, model checking procedure to verify the local properties and he then needs only to demonstrate the certification of the local requirements of the component to the manufacturer. Hence there is no need for suppliers to provide full ECU specifications to the manufacturer.

Compositional verification is still not easy enough to use because of the complete set of properties required to proof the specification on the higher hierarchy level. Completing the property set for each component is time consuming and tedious, a problem that ongoing research trys to alleviate.

4   Closing the Gap Between Models and Systems

If for reasons of cost, space or time an implementation is not generated with a certified code generator, then there is a gap in the formal chain from the model to the actual implemented system. Testing is a way to bridge that gap, but it is time-consuming, costly and incomplete. Again formal verification significantly helps to improve the testing process by complementing any set of test vectors, which might be set up by e.g. heuristical approaches. Technically this Automatic Test vector Generation (ATG) [24] first computes the coverage obtained by the existing test vector set so far. Remaining test goals such as uncovered code, states, conditions, output signals etc. are derived from this analysis and automatically specified for the model checker. Iteratively the model checker now looks for and finds a test vector for each remaining test goal. Since by chance with each new test vector, also other test goals might already have been covered already, after each iteration the coverage analysis computes the set of uncovered test goals so that no test goal is computed twice by the modelchecker. Since the modelchecker always finds a test vector for a test goal if there is any, the progress of this procedure is guaranteed until the targeted test vector coverage is reached, even if it should be the entire model.

These test vectors can then be used for conformance testing of e.g. Hardware In the Loop (HIL) and for regression testing as shown in figure 4.

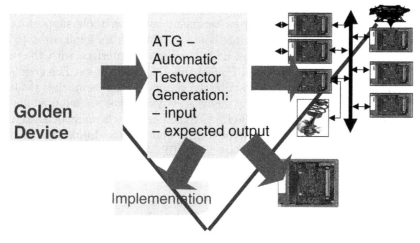

Fig. 4. Advanced Verification Technology

5   Enhancing Trust in Fault-Tree Analysis

Fault-tree analysis (FTA) is a widely adopted technique to systematically analyze causes for a given failure of a complex system. Traditionally, a fault tree
is constructed top-down based on knowledge about the structure of the system
and the interaction of subsystems. With the increasing system complexity and
the accompanying introduction of model-based development techniques in the
industrial process, a substantial amount of this knowledge is laid down in the
system models. But there are several issues with classical FTA:

Coherency:
- How do models used for safety analysis relate to the actual design?
- How can safety engineers keep track with ongoing developments in the
  design models?

Plausibility:
- How can a system designer relate a cut-set to "her" model?
- How can she understand, how the cut-set can arise?

Accuracy: How can
- mission phases
- numerical thresholds
... be assessed without gross over-approximation?

Completeness:
- How can a safety designer assert that all minimal cut-sets have been
  identified?

The ESACS project[10] (Enhanced Safety Assessment of Complex Systems)
addresses these topics. The technical and scientific objectives of ESACS are to

---

[10] http://www.cert.fr/esacs/

define a methodology to improve the safety analysis practice for complex systems development, to set up a shared environment based on tools supporting the methodology, and to validate the methodology through its application to case studies. Figure 5 shows where the ESACS approach interface with the safety process as it is described in the ARP 4654 and 4761 documents. The grey boxes on the right side of the diagram describe the system development while the boxes on the left represent different safety analysis activities that are required in order to develop a certifiable aircraft. The ESACS methodology is main focussed in the area of "Development of System Architecture" and "System Implementation" on the development side and the interface to the PSSA (Preliminary System Safety Analysis) and SSA (System Safety Analysis).

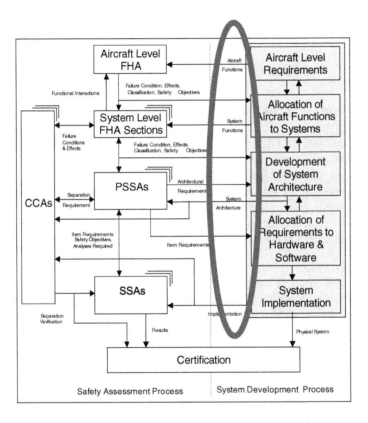

Fig. 5. The ESACS approach towards ARP 4754 and 4761

The ESACS project developed a common methodology for model based safety analysis. The Analysis can start with system model or conceptional design model that implements the nominal behavior of the system. The first step is to verify that this model is correct with respect to the given safety requirements. In the next step the nominal system behavior is enriched by failure-modes. The failures can be selected from a library of common failure patterns that has been developed in conjunction with the industrial partners. A more detailed description of the ESACS methodology can be found in [25].

Each technology provider in ESACS implemented a vertical "line", i.e. an instantiation of the ESACS methodology. Our "implementation line" (STSA – **St**atemate **S**afety **A**nalysis) is based on the modeling tool Statemate. The first step when doing an automatic safety analysis is to execute a set of simple robustness checks (e.g. to find non-determinism and write/write or read/write races) with the already mentioned ModelChecker. After that it should be ensured that the nominal model fulfills all safety requirements. When these preliminary steps have been taken care of, the actual fault-tree analysis can start with the definition of the top-level event (TLE). Simple properties can be defined directly in the STSA. More complex safety requirements can be imported from the ModelCertifier.

The injection of failure-modes into the the design model is done by automatically introducing new input variables that switch between nominal and failure behaviour. After that we use a BDD based model-checker to compute a parameterized reachabilty, i.e. for each state in the reachable set we keep a complete history of all the failure-modes that have been activated. Using this information we extract all minmal sets of failure-modes that are necessary to cause the TLE.

The analysis results can be exported to the commercial FaultTree+ tool (Isograph) for further evaluation (e.g. quantitative analysis). Often it is not sufficient to know which failures contribute to a failure scenario but also what is the exact system behavior leading to this situation. For this purpose the STSA tool can generate an an SCP (simulation control program) for each cut-set. This SCP can be used together with the Statemate Simulator to drive the system model directly to the top-level event.

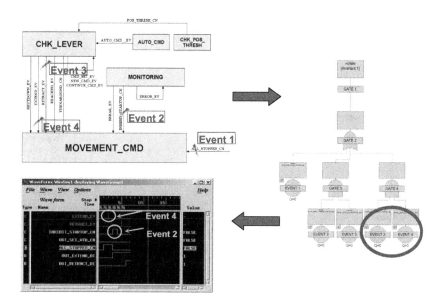

Fig. 6. The ESACS approach towards ARP 4754 and 4761

The automatic FTA implemented in the STSA tool has been evaluated using two case studies. The SPS (secondary power system) case study was provided by Alenia Aeronautica. There have been several instances of the same basic model that mainly differed in complexity. The second case-study, provided by Airbus, was a design model of a controller for the High-Lift System of the Airbus A340 aircraft. A detailed description of the applied techniques and the results can be found in [26].

It has been found that through the use of abstraction, automatic FTA is feasible even on very complex systems. Furthermore it has been shown that the abstraction technique is safe, i.e. no combination of failures that can lead to the TLE is missed. However it is possible that the analysis results are too pessimistic due to the set of failures that causes the TLE in the abstracted model is smaller than for the original model.

6 SafeAir

In the SafeAir project the goal was to improve the V based development process to save development time and effort while preserving or improving the dependability of the developed systems. The implementation methodology that is developed in SafeAir increases the understandability and correctness of the requirements, the correctness of the design and the code with respect to the requirements. The emphasis within the project was on formal development of systems, providing formal specification, model checking technology, automatic test case generation and validated code generation.

The semantic integration of system-level and design-level modeling tools allows a virtually integrated V-process that is sharpened up to a Y-based process with the required steps at the bottom of the former V being considerably automated. See figure 7.

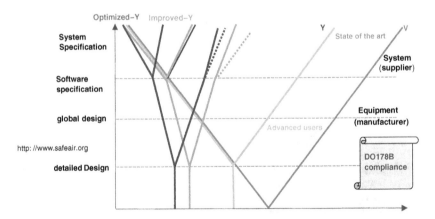

Fig. 7. Improving V based processes - lessons from SafeAir. Diagram by Mr. Pilarski, Airbus France.

Automatic code generation for the complete integrated system with a certified code generator complying to the DO178B standard eliminates manual code generation and integration as well as unit testing on the Code level. Formal verification partially supersedes testing by proving the correctness of the design at multiple levels ranging from subcomponents for creating golden devices up to the overall virtually integrated system. Technically using the generated C code for verification, even formal verification of the target C code is possible, though not required since code generation can always be automatically validated if needed. For a certain C compiler automatic code validation can even be applied to the binary representation, proving the correctness of each translation. Remaining test cases not covered by verification or validation are finally addressed by automatic generation of test cases, which could additionally be used to fortify verification results.

The modeling tools being integrated in SafeAir are Statemate, Simulink / Stateflow, SCADE and Sildex, with the latter two constituting the possible integration platforms being able to import any of the formats mentioned, enabling the use of best-in-class problem-specific COTS modeling tools for central aspects such as control law design or architectural design. See figure 8.

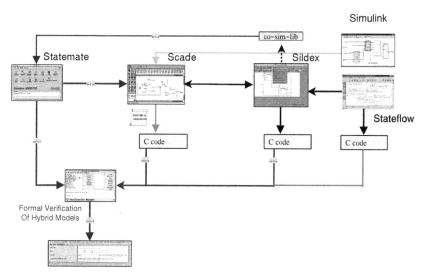

Fig. 8. Integration of Modeling Tools in SafeAir

The integration is realized by gateways that translate models from the various formats to semantically equivalent representations in either SCADE or Sildex. For Statemate the translation to SCADE is integrated in the Statemate tool and even an interface for co-simulation is available.

Apart from the possibility to verify models with respect to their SCADE representation, we are able to verify models in each language representation also either directly or by using a C code generator shipped with or dedicated to the specific CASE tools. For example Stateflow verification through the TargetLink code generator was realized outside the SafeAir project in cooperation with DaimlerChrysler.

The application cases have demonstrated that this new methodology should significantly reduce the risk of design errors and shorten the overall design cycle compared to a traditional development.

The project demonstrated that the goal to produce an open environment, its methodology and training material, to develop embedded software for safety critical systems that supports multi formalisms, simulation and animation, formal verification and automatic qualified code generation is achievable and industrially viable.

7   Conclusion

Numerous modeling issues have been identified and addressed using formal methods throughout the whole design process. We have presented different application scenarios in which formal verification techniques can significantly alleviate the typical problems in each of the resp. design phases. All presented approaches use model checking techniques to complement deficiencies of or even replace conventional techniques, leading to faster and cheaper development of more reliable automotive applications as the SafeAir project in the avionics domain has already shown.

Except for the use case of virtual integration test & IP protection all outlined techniques have already found their way to a commercial product being available on the market[11].

References

1. Damm, W., Schulte, C., Segelken, M., Wittke, H., Higgen, U., Eckrich, M.: Formale verifikation von ascet modellen im rahmen der entwicklung der aktivlenkung. Lecuture Notes in Informatics **P-34** (2003) 340–345
2. Baufreton, P., Dupont, F., Lesergent, T., Segelken, M., Brinkmann, H., Strichman, O., Winkelmann, K.: Safeair: Advanced design tools for aircraft systems and airborne software. In: Proceedings of the 2001 International Conference on Dependable Systems and Networks. (2001)
3. Clarke, E.M., Grumberg, O., Peled, D.A.: Model Checking. MIT Press,Cambridge, Massachusets, London, England (1999) ISBN 0-262-03270-8.
4. Owre, S., Rushby, J.M., Shankar, N.: PVS: A Prototype Verification System. In Kapur, D., ed.: 11th International Conference on Automated Deduction. Volume 607 of LNAI., Saratoga Springs, New York, USA, Springer-Verlag (1992) 748–752
5. Paulson, L.C.: Isabelle: a generic theorem prover. Volume 828 of Lecture Notes in Computer Science. Springer-Verlag (1994)
6. Hunt Jr., W.A., Somenzi, F., eds.: Computer Aided Verification, 15th International Conference, CAV 2003, Boulder, Colorado, USA, July 8 – 12, 2003, Proceedings. In Hunt Jr., W.A., Somenzi, F., eds.: Computer aided verification (CAV 2003). Lecture Notes in Computer Science, Springer Verlag (2003)

---

[11] see www.osc-es.de

7. Maler, O., Pnueli, A., eds.: Hybrid Systems: Computation and Control (HSCC '03). In Maler, O., Pnueli, A., eds.: Hybrid Systems: Computation and Control (HSCC '03). Lecture Notes in Computer Science, Springer Verlag (2003)
8. Bienmüller, T., Damm, W., Wittke, H.: The STATEMATE verification environment – making it real. In Emerson, E.A., Sistla, A.P., eds.: 12th International Conference on Computer Aided Verification, CAV. Number 1855 in Lecture Notes in Computer Science, Springer-Verlag (2000) 561–567
9. Bryant, R.E.: Graph-based algorithms for Boolean function manipulation. IEEE Transactions on Computers **C-35** (1986) 677–691
10. Coudert, O., Berthet, C., Madre, J.: Verification of synchronous sequential machines based on symbolic execution. In: Automatic Verification Methods for Finite State Systems. Volume 407 of LNCS., Springer Verlag (1989) 365–373
11. Stalmarck, G., Sflund, M.: Modeling and verifying systems and software in propositional logic. In Daniels, B.K., ed.: Safety of Computer Control Systems (SAFE-COMP'90), Pergamon Press (1990) 31–36
12. Moskewicz, M.W., Madigan, C.F., Zhao, Y., Zhang, L., Malik, S.: Chaff: Engineering an Efficient SAT Solver. In: Proceedings of the 38th Design Automation Conference (DAC'01). (2001)
13. Filliâtre, J.C., Owre, S., Rueß, H., Shankar, N.: ICS: Integrated canonizer and solver. In Berry, G., Comon, H., Finkel, A., eds.: Proceedings of the 13th International Conference on Computer Aided Verification (Paris, France). Volume 2102 of Lecture Notes in Computer Science., Springer Verlag (2001) 246–249
14. Stump, A., Barrett, C., Dill, D.: CVC: a cooperating validity checker. In Godskesen, J.C., ed.: Proceedings of the International Conference on Computer-Aided Verification. Lecture Notes in Computer Science (2002)
15. Shankar, N.: Combining theorem proving and model checking through symbolic analysis. In: 11th International Conference on Concurrency Theory (CONCUR). Volume 1877 of Lecture Notes in Computer Science., University Park, USA, Springer-Verlag (2000) 1–16
16. Basin, D., Friedrich, S.: Combining WS1S and HOL. In: Frontiers of Combining Systems 2 (FROCOS). Research Studies Press/Wiley (2002) 39–56
17. Bemporad, A., Morari, M.: Verification of hybrid systems via mathematical programming. In Vaandrager, F.W., van Schuppen, J.H., eds.: Hybrid Systems: Computation and Control (HSCC'99). Volume 1569 of Lecture Notes in Computer Science., Springer Verlag (1999) 31–45
18. Clarke, E., Grumberg, O., Jha, S., Lu, Y., Veith, H.: Counterexample-guided abstraction refinement. In Emerson, E., Sistla, A., eds.: Computer Aided Verification. Volume 1855 of Lecture Notes in Computer Science., Springer Verlag (2000) 154–169
19. Glusman, M., Kamhi, G., Mador-Haim, S., Fraer, R., Vardi, M.: Multiple-counterexample guided iterative abstraction refinement: An industrial evaluation. In Garavel, H., Hatcliff, J., eds.: Tools and Algorithms for the Construction and Analysis of Systems. Volume 2619 of Lecture Notes in Computer Science., Springer Verlag (2003) 176–191
20. S. Graf, H. Saidi: Construction of abstract state graphs with PVS. In Grumberg, O., ed.: Proc. 9th INternational Conference on Computer Aided Verification (CAV'97). Volume 1254., Springer Verlag (1997) 72–83
21. Ball, T., Majumdar, R., Millstein, T., Rajamani, S.K.: Automatic predicate abstraction of C programs. SIGPLAN Notices **36** (2001) 203–213 Proceedings of PLDI 2001.

22. Becker, B., Behle, M., Eisenbrand, F., Fränzle, M., Herbstritt, M., Herde, C., Hoffmann, J., Kröning, D., Nebel, B., Polian, I., Wimmer, R.: Bounded model checking and inductive verification of hybrid discrete-continuous systems. In: ITG/GI/GMM-Workshop "Methoden und Beschreibungssprachen zur Modellierung und Verifikation von Schaltungen und Systemen". (2004)

23. Bienmüller, T., Brockmeyer, U., Damm, W., Döhmen, G., Eßmann, C., Holberg, H.J., Hungar, H., Josko, B., Schlör, R., Wittich, G., Wittke, H., Clements, G., Rowlands, J., Sefton, E.: Formal Verification of an Avionics Application using Abstraction and Symbolic Model Checking. In Redmill, F., Anderson, T., eds.: Towards System Safety – Proceedings of the Seventh Safety-critical Systems Symposium, Huntingdon, UK, Safety-Critical Systems Club, SV (1999) 150–173

24. Bohn, J., Damm, W., Klose, J., Moik, A., Wittke, H.: Modeling and validating train system applications using statemate and live sequence charts. In Ertas, A., Ehrig, H., Krämer, B.J., eds.: Proceedings of the Conference on Integrated Design and Process Technology (IDPT2002), Society for Design and Process Science (2002)

25. Bozzano, M., et al.: Esacs: An integrated methodology for design and safety analysis of complex systems. ESREL (2003)

26. Bretschneider, M., Holberg, H.J., Böde, E., Brückner, I., Peikenkamp, T., Spenke, H.: Model-based safety analysis of a flap control system. INCOSE (2004)

Automotive Software: A Challenge and Opportunity for Model-Based Software Development

Gabor Karsai

Institute for Software Integrated Systems
Vanderbilt University, P.O. Box 1829 Sta. B.
Nashville, TN 37235, USA
gabor.karsai@vanderbilt.edu

Abstract. Embedded software development for automotive applications is widely considered as a significant source of innovation and improvements in cars. However, software development processes do not address well the needs of large-scale distributed real-time systems, like the ones automobiles do (or soon will) contain. The paper introduces a vision for the model-based development of embedded software, which is based on the broad-spectrum modeling of the applications in the context of a larger system, formal (and computer-supported) analysis of models, and automatic synthesis of the application(s). The paper also describes some initial steps taken to build the infrastructure for supporting such a process in the form of modeling and model transformation tools. The paper concludes with a list of challenging research problems.

1 Introduction

Our everyday vehicles are turning into complex, distributed and real-time embedded systems (DRE). The trends are clear: new functions are more economical to implement in software running on a networked processor than in a dedicated hardware, and thus Electronic Control Units (ECU) and software implementations proliferate.

It is common knowledge that large-scale, distributed real-time embedded systems are notoriously hard to build. With the best of intentions, suppliers develop their software components, which perfectly satisfy the design requirements, yet when integration comes, the system is unstable and unreliable. Even worse: it is impossible to figure out what causes the problems. All participants followed well-established processes and the components meet their requirements, yet the integrated system is unusable. However, this is not a failure of individual ingredients (i.e. the components, the architecture, the platform, the scheduling algorithms, the hardware), but it is a breakdown on the system level: a *systemic failure*. When the perfect pieces are put together, the result is imperfect.

Arguably, at the core of this problem is a not well-understood phenomenon of subtle interactions among components. System architects of embedded systems must ask questions like: given a component A increases it production rate of data blocks by 100%, how will it impact the timing and performance of a component B located on a

M. Broy, I.H. Krüger, and M. Meisinger (Eds.): ASWSD 2004, LNCS 4147, pp. 103–115, 2006.
© Springer-Verlag Berlin Heidelberg 2006

processor which also hosts a component C that is a consumer of A's data? All embedded system developers are familiar with scenarios like these, yet analytical or other approaches are rarely used in design time to answer these questions.

We need an approach: an *engineering process* to address these issues. The process must be based on (1) modeling of the embedded system to be created, (2) analysis and verification of the models, and (3) synthesis and integration of the system from the models. We assume that an embedded system (ES) is a computer-based system consisting of hardware *and* software components, embedded in a physical environment, which imposes strict timing requirements on the product. Below, we describe the vision of a model-based [1] engineering process and its various stages.

2   Model-Based Engineering and Development of Embedded Software

The engineering and development approach envisioned below supports the construction and evolution of embedded software, and it heavily relies on the use of models: models of the software as well as the environment in which the software operates. As such, it advocates an approach similar to that of the Model-Driven Architecture (MDA) of OMG [4]. However, it extends and specializes that vision to the domain of embedded software, which operates in a physical environment and whose design decisions have a physical impact (literally). The notional process is outlined on Figure 1.

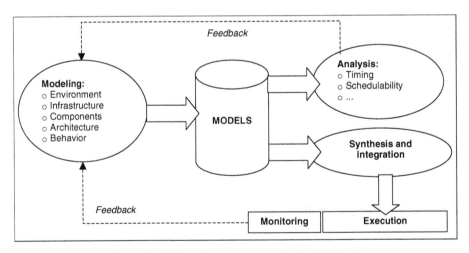

Fig. 1. Model-based Development of Embedded Software

Stage I: Modeling
The engineering process starts with a modeling phase. In the modeling phase, the system designer creates models of the system and its environment. These models constitute the *design documentation* of the system, and they should, at least, include:

- The environment models capture the assumptions made about the environment of the system. The requirement for the environmental models is that they should *capture all relevant assumptions* that could impact the system's behavior. Examples include: all the "sensors" and "actuators" in the system, interrupt sources and their expected rates, ranges for values of sensors and actuators, absolute physical limits on physical variables, etc. In the automotive domain an example could be the dynamic model of the engine (as it is needed for the engine control software).

- The infrastructure models capture how the software-hardware platform works what the ES will be run on. The requirement for the infrastructure models is that they should be *predictive*: i.e. they should be able to forecast the ultimate dynamic behavior of the platform under varying computational load requirements. Example: qualitative/quantitative model(s) of the RTOS the embedded system is running on. In the automotive domain a specific example would be a detailed model of the OSEK implementation used.

- The components models capture how the individual components (concurrent objects) could be interfaced with and how they behave. The requirement for the component models is that they should be *usable in analysis*: given an assembly of components on a given infrastructure, we want to be able to compute the dynamic behavior of the ensemble. Example: a model of a component in terms of its interface, the timing properties associated with those interfaces, the externally observable behavior of the component when the interfaces are activated, etc. In the automotive domain a specific example would be the model of the components that implement an electronic automatic transmission system.

- The architecture models capture how the system is put together from the components and how it is mapped to the platform. The requirement for the architectural model is that it should *contribute to the analysis* of the models: we must be able to compute the behavior of the system from the models of the components, the infrastructure and the platform. Example: if the application is constructed from components that are scheduled according to the rules of dataflow scheduling (i.e. data-driven control flow), then a model could be the component connectivity diagram. In the automotive domain an example here is the full architectural model of a cooperative cruise control application.

- The behavior models capture the overall, expected dynamic behavior of the embedded systems. The requirement for behavioral models is that they faithfully *capture the expected dynamics* of the system, observable on its external and internal interfaces. Example: end-to-end latency between sensors and actuators, expected behavior of the system in "value space" and in "temporal space", safety constraints on the values and the timing of those values produced by the system, etc. In the automotive domain the example here would be the model of the expected dynamics of the automatic transmission (e.g. "it should never 'hunt', i.e. oscillate rapidly between two gears" — expressed in a precise, mathematical form).

Arguably, there is no single modeling language currently available that can support all these modeling aspects. Note that state-of-the-art architecture description languages support only some of the aspects, not all. ADL-s tend to focus on software artifacts only, however (1) embedded systems include significant hardware components, and (2) embedded software operates in a physical environment that impacts and is impacted by the software design. However, experience shows that all the above models are needed: their lack indicates the lack of understanding by the system's designer. As such, new, domain-specific modeling languages (DSML) are necessary [22] that support the modeling of the above aspects [3].

It is a highly relevant question to ask how these models are related to code and how model-based development is related to traditional, code-based development. We argue that models should be representations (or abstractions) of the code, and should be kept "in sync" with code. This does not necessarily mean that a model-code automatic linkage is necessary (as it is often done today in many model-based tools) rather the model of the code must be maintained together with the code. Skilled developers will always develop excellent code that would be impossible to reproduce using models and generators, but where models are useful: system level composition and analysis, the model-based approach has clear advantages.

Note that DSML-s are closely related to the concept of domain-specific architectures (DSSA): they offer a framework in which domain-specific applications can be built. The difference is that while DSSA offer an architectural solution (which has to be instantiated and customized through programming for specific applications), DSML-s offer a linguistic solution (in the form of modeling languages, which can be used to model and construct the application).

Stage II: Analysis

Once models are created various analysis studies shall be performed. The goal of the analysis is to verify through various means, like simulation, model checking, and theorem proving, etc., that the DRE will meet its expectations if built—according to the models. We believe this stage is crucial in the development process: this step must provide assurances that if the system is built as described by the model, and the assumptions about the components, the infrastructure, and the environment are true, then the system will work as expected, i.e. exhibits the desired behavior. This is one crucial step in embedded software development: as the consequences of failures are high and potential faults are hard to reproduce, engineering analysis must be done before testing and deployment.

The analysis has to be able to predict the behavior of the system, based on the models of system: the components, the architecture, the infrastructure, and its environment. This predictive property is an essential requirement for analysis: the tools must be able to compute the behavior of the system and match it up to the expected dynamic behavior. Furthermore, they should also be able to provide formal proofs that the system is logically correct, and provide assurances that the computation of the system dynamics is sound.

Note that the analysis is necessarily based on the models of the system, and not necessarily on the code. This makes analysis simple(r), but puts a burden on the developer: the models must provide an accurate representation of the implementation code. Note also that the analysis allows early verification of the designs, even if code is not available, only the models of the components. Assuming that the analysis is correct, the main requirement for the component developer is to design and build components that comply with the models, and the system will work as expected.

The ultimate goal in model-based embedded systems is that the analysis perfectly predicts the system's behavior —without actually building the system. This may not be feasible because of inherent inaccuracies in the models or lack of knowledge about details. However, we shall aim for, as a minimum, analysis techniques that will pinpoint potential problems in the design when implemented on the platform and give an early indication, well before integration.

This step requires analysis tools, however an analysis tool may not be immediately applicable if it can treat models only in its own, domain-specific modeling language. If a tool does not "understand" the models built in the first stage then it has to be integrated with the modeling tools used there. The core concept of integration is *semantic interoperability*: models expressed in a domain-specific modeling language must have an *equivalent semantics* in the language of the analysis tool(s). Furthermore, analysis problems ("queries") and results ("replies") should also be translated between the modeling and the analysis tools, as the designer would expect to be able to pose questions and receive answers in the domain-specific language of the design, not that of the analysis tool. This type of a semantic interoperation is a complex and difficult requirement for the model-based development, but it is unavoidable.

Stage III: Synthesis and Integration
Having the design verified by analysis, the process continues with the synthesis and integration stage. By "synthesis" we mean activities that produce ingredients of the implementation from the models automatically, and by "integration" we mean all the activities that compose the components (at compile-time or at run-time) leading to a fully functional system.

First, the components are built, perhaps using generative programming techniques [10] or hand coding. Once components are created, they have to be instrumented, executed and verified against their models. If necessary, the models have to be revised and the process iterated using the new models.

Next, the system implementation has to be synthesized from the architectural models. The synthesis can be implemented as a set of transformations [20] that map the design models into artifacts running on the infrastructure.

The integration should be done first on an instrumented platform that allows capturing the behavior of the running system in a form that is representative of the dynamics: the time-domain behavior of system. The instrumentation can be implemented in the form of strategically placed "software sensors" that report significant events in the system. The data provided by the instrumentation should be compared against data generated in the analysis phase, and if differences are found the design need to be revised, and the process must iterate. The discrepancies found at this stage are indicative of some requirements not having been met, i.e. the design is faulty. The designer then shall modify the design: modify the architecture, introduce new components, change component characteristics, choose another platform, etc. This model update is perhaps the most difficult step of the process, as it is not clear how to explain differences and which model must be changed to remove the discrepancy. However, if the implementation is created through formal transformations, there is some hope that the observed system dynamics can be "projected back" into the design models, and thus the discrepancies explained in terms of the models. This is a conjecture at this point and it needs to be proven.

Tool Support

A suite of integrated tools is needed to support the above process. Tools exist today that support some steps in the process. However, these tools often work in isolation, using their own proprietary language(s) hence there is a strong need for tool integration. Tool integration should support *semantic interoperability*: the meaningful interchange of data among the tools [16]. In a minimal process, the modeling, analysis, and synthesis tools should be tied together such that they form a seamless toolchain supporting the process. Large-scale processes involving multiple engineers at different sites should be aided by web-based open tool integration frameworks that facilitate sharing models across the enterprise.

3 Modeling and Model Transformations

The above vision for the model-based development of embedded systems presupposes the existence of technology that allows: (1) the definition of domain-specific modeling languages, (2) the editing and manipulation of domain-specific models, (3) and the transformation of models between different modeling approaches while preserving the semantic content of those models.

We have built a meta-programmable visual modeling environment, GME (see [2] for details), to solve the problem of defining and editing DSML-s. For specifying the abstract syntax of DSML-s, GME provides a UML class diagram [7] editor that allows capture of the abstract syntax in the form of a diagram, and of the static semantics in the form of OCL [15] expressions. Note that the UML class diagram acts like a "grammar" whose sentences are the "object graphs" that comply with it. For concrete syntax, GME uses idioms (patterns over classes) and stereotypes: specific idioms and stereotypes have specific meaning for the GME visualization and editing engine. As GME has a well-defined set of visualization tools but these will probably need to be extended in the future such that arbitrary visualization (and manipulation) techniques could be coupled to entities in the abstract syntax. Once the abstract and concrete syntax are defined, i.e. the meta-model of the language is built GME can "interpret" this metamodel and morph itself into a domain-specific GME that supports that (and only that) language. This GME instance strictly enforces the language "rules": only models that comply with the abstract syntax and the static semantics can be built. This happens at model-editing time: the designer is warned about constraint violations.

The semantics of DSML-s can be defined by a mapping between the abstract syntax and a semantic domain [21]. For the mapping into the semantic domain we have chosen a pragmatic approach: we assume that there is always a "target platform" whose semantics is well known. This approach has been used in the past for formally specifying semantics [13]. Furthermore, the target platform also has an abstract syntax (with static semantics), and the transformation between the domain-specific models and target platform models establishes the semantics of the DSML-s in terms of the target models.

We have created a meta-programmable tool for implementing model transformations [10]: GRE (for Graph Rewriting Engine). GRE is programmed through a high-level language, called GReAT (Graph Rewriting And Transformations) captures metamodels of transformations as explicitly sequenced graph rewriting rules (see [10][11] for details). A graph rewriting rule consists of a graph pattern (which is matched against an input graph), a guard condition (which is evaluated over the matched subgraph), a consequence pattern (which captures what objects must be created in the target graph), and a set of attribute mapping actions (which describe how to compute the attributes of target objects from the attributes of input objects). The rewriting rules are transforming the source models (i.e. the input "graph") into the target models (i.e. the output "graph"). They explicitly reference elements of the source and the target metamodels, that is the pattern and consequence nodes of the transformation steps are strictly typed. Also, the input (target) subgraphs mentioned in the rules must be compliant with the input (target) metamodels. For efficiency reasons rewriting rules accept "pivot" points: initial bindings for pattern variables. This reduces the search in the pattern matching process (effectively reducing it to matching on a rooted tree). One can also explicitly sequence the execution of the rules, and sequential, parallel, and conditional composition of the rules is also available. GRE works as an interpreter: it executes transformation programs (which are expressed in the form of transformation models) on domain-specific models to generate target models. Obviously it runs slowly, although it can provide help in debugging transformation programs. We have also created a code generator that compiles the transformation specifications into executable code

Figure 2 shows how GRE works and the relationships between source and target models and their metamodels. In order to set up a specific modeling and model transformation process one has to create metamodels for the (input) source domain, the (output) target domain, and for the transformations. One can then use the meta-programmable modeling tool (GME) to create and edit domain models, and the meta-programmable transformation tool (GRE and GReAT) to transform the models into

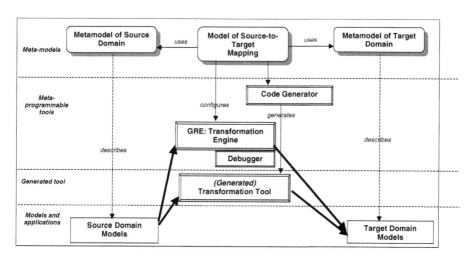

Fig. 2. Tools for the definition, manipulation, and transformation of domain-specific models

target models. If the speed of the transformation is a concern, the code generator can be used to translate the transformation models into executable code.

We believe a crucial ingredient in the above scheme is the meta-programmable transformation tool that executes a transformation metamodel (as a "program") and facilitates the model transformation. Using the concepts and techniques of graph transformations allows not only the formal specification of transformations, but, arguably, also reasoning about the properties of the transformations.

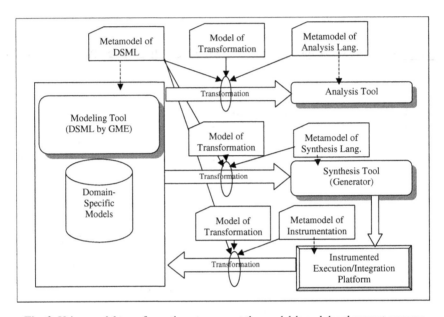

Fig. 3. Using model transformations to support the model-based development process

Figure 3 illustrates how the model transformation technology could be used to facilitate the envisioned model-based development process. Note how metamodels are used to define the domain-specific modeling language for system modeling, the language for the analysis tool, the language for the synthesis tool, and the language for instrumentation. Transformation models, defined in terms of their source and target metamodels could be directly executed (using the GRE engine), or compiled into code (using the code generator). Thus, model transformation technology facilitates tool integration among the various tools needed in a model-based embedded system development process.

The tool architecture described above goes beyond the current state-of-the-art through placing emphasis on the use of the domain-specific languages, but in itself does not solve the complexity problem: it merely establishes a foundation for building a tool infrastructure. In industrial practice today automotive systems are often developed in the Simulink/Stateflow environment that offers *one* approach for model-driven development. We believe that in the next generation of tools we need better, more "domain-oriented" languages, precisely defined semantics ("models of computation") for the concurrent objects applications will be built from, and tighter connection with formal (not only simulation-based) analysis of systems.

4 Research Issues

As of today, the model-based development process envisioned and outlined above is not fully realized yet. Some core technologies already exist, but additional work is needed. Below is an initial list of research problems that need to be solved:

o   What are the domain-specific modeling languages that allow the broad-spectrum modeling of embedded systems as described above? How do we model the environment, the infrastructure (i.e. the "platform"), in addition to the components, architecture and the behavior?
There are some active efforts (e.g. SAE AADL, or AutoSAR) that work towards architecture modeling and analysis, but the activity should be extended towards modeling architectures in conjunction with (at least assumptions about) the physical environment the systems operate in.

o   How can these languages support modeling complex applications and the interactions between systems? How can a (relatively) small number of designers build large and complex models whose fidelity is sufficient to make predictions about (and foresee problems in) complex designs?
Modeling languages and their tools must have mechanisms for managing complexity (e.g. modularization, version control), but they should also be acceptable and usable by domain experts and engineers. These people need "model engineering" environments, not software development environments.

o   What are the techniques and tools that allow the analysis of large-scale, multi-domain models? If analysis is too complex, how can one abstract the models into a "simpler" form that can be analyzed?
The performance of analysis and verification tools is a particular concern. Scalability to real-life systems is an issue, and further research is needed on automatic verification such that it can tackle complex, including adaptive, systems. The modeling, analysis, and management of effects of faults in systems are other highly relevant and critical issues.

o   How to translate design domain-specific properties into analysis domain specific properties that the analysis tools can understand? How can the results of the analysis translated back into the design domain?

o   What are the portions of the system implementation that can be synthesized from models and how? How to introduce para-functional properties, like cost, into the synthesis such that expectations for the final system are automatically met?
If model transformations or automatic code generation is used, they need to be "resource-aware", i.e. they should generate deployable artifacts (e.g. code) that are guaranteed to satisfy system-level requirements. The topic of resource-aware transformations is a promising area of further research.

o   How to instrument the embedded application such that the observations made on the running system can be fed back into the design process? How to interpret the observations and inform the designer about necessary changes?

5 Related Work

In recent years significant amount of work has been done in areas that are relevant for the research issues outlined above.

First, many aspects of UML 2.0 [5] are focusing on issues relevant for embedded system applications. In fact, the "real-time profile" (called the "Schedulability, Performance, Timing" profile [6]) for UML, clearly addresses a number of questions related to embedded systems. However, UML profiles are specific idioms for use within the UML, and thus they do not define a brand new DSML. Furthermore, they do not model the (physical) environment and its impact on the system's behavior. For instance, environment-imposed timing, latency, or event rate attributes are rarely captured in UML. The importance of platform modeling has been recognized and some initial work has started [17], but many problems are still open.

The model-based development of complex embedded applications today is done using a few tools, the most relevant being Mathworks' Simulink/Stateflow. However, the industrial practice rarely involves formal analysis and verification is based on testing [18]. There are a number of tools for analyzing hybrid systems [26][27][28], however the scalability is an issue. For practical systems the tools need to have automatic abstraction capabilities.

Early experiments with translating Simulink/Stateflow models into hybrid automata for analysis [29] show the feasibility of the approach but it is not ready for industrial scale use yet. Synthesis from high-level method is farther advanced. For instance, Leue's work on Message Sequence Charts (MSC) [8] and Harel's work on Live Sequence Charts [9] illustrates how systems could be synthesized from high-level models. Similar results have been developed by Whittle [23], Krueger [24], and Systä [25].

For distributed real-time systems, monitoring-based debugging is a well-established field [30], however further research work is needed on how to couple it to the model-based development process for embedded systems. Recent advances in model-based testing [31] point to relevant work.

As the complexity of automotive embedded systems grows, techniques from large-scale software engineering practice need to be incorporated into the development process. For example, rapid prototyping, software product lines, architecture mappings from models, and software factories [32] are some, but not the only, relevant and related areas.

While there is significant progress in the area of tools, it is probably fair to say is that today most embedded systems are still developed in procedural languages, using a real-time operating system. More advanced, more model-based development happens using control-oriented visual modeling/simulation and code generation tools (e.g. Matrix-X or Simulink/Stateflow). Model verification and analysis is still very simple, mostly because of scalability problems in the tools developed by the research community. The verification tools need become more robust and scalable to be accepted in the industrial community.

No doubt, there is no, and probably never will be, a single overarching tool that can verify everything about an embedded system design and a suite of tools are needed. (This seems to be the experience from the VLSI/CAD field as well.) Furthermore, design languages will be probably very different from the analysis/verification languages, and thus model transformations are necessary to build the bridge between design and analysis, as well as synthesis. In a bigger sense, even if industrial-grade tools are available, tool integration is still a significant problem that needs to be solved.

6   Conclusions

To conclude, we have to emphasize the fact that the design of complex, large-scale real-time embedded systems (like the ones we find in automobiles) is a difficult task. It is difficult because software design cannot be done in isolation from physical considerations, and thus an integrated view is needed. We believe that having models and motivating the designers to think in terms of these models to analyze and understand the design is the right first step towards creating a new development process that can address today's and tomorrow's needs.

Acknowledgements

The NSF ITR on "Foundations of Hybrid and Embedded Software Systems" has supported, in part, the activities described in this paper. DARPA, AFRL, and USAF also sponsored the effort, under agreement number F30602-00-1-0580.The US Government is authorized to reproduce and distribute reprints for Governmental purposes notwithstanding any copyright thereon. The views and conclusions contained therein are those of authors and should not be interpreted as necessarily representing the official policies and endorsements, either expressed or implied, of the DARPA, the AFRL or the US Government.

References

[1] J. Sztipanovits, and G. Karsai, "Model-Integrated Computing", Computer, Apr. 1997, pp. 110-112

[2] Ledeczi, et al., "Composing Domain-Specific Design Environments", Computer, Nov. 2001, pp. 44-51.

[3] Karsai, G., Sztipanovits, J., Ledeczi, A., Bapty, T.: "Model-Integrated Development of Embedded Software," Proceedings of the IEEE, Vol. 91, No.1., pp. 145-164, January, 2003

[4] Model-driven Architecture, http://www.omg.org/mda/

[5] UML 2.0 information http://www.uml.org/#UML2.0

[6] UML SPT Profile http://www.omg.org/cgi-bin/doc?formal/2005-01-02

[7] J. Rumbaugh, I. Jacobson, and G. Booch, "The Unified Modeling Language Reference Manual", Addison-Wesley, 1998.

[8] S. Leue, L. Mehrmann and M. Rezai, Synthesizing ROOM Models from Message Sequence Chart Specifications, Technical Report 98-06, Dept. of Electrical and Computer Engineering, University of Waterloo, April 1998.

[9] David Harel, Hillel Kugler: Synthesizing State-Based Object Systems from LSC Specifications. Int. J. Found. Comput. Sci. 13(1): 5-51 (2002).

[10] Agrawal A., Levendovszky T., Sprinkle J., Shi F., Karsai G., "Generative Programming via Graph Transformations in the Model-Driven Architecture", Workshop on Generative Techniques in the Context of Model Driven Architecture, OOPSLA , Nov. 5, 2002, Seattle, WA.

[11] Grzegorz Rozenberg, "Handbook of Graph Grammars and Computing by Graph Transformation", World Scientific Publishing Co. Pte. Ltd., 1997.

[12] Blostein D., Schürr A., "Computing with Graphs and Graph Rewriting", Technical Report AIB 97-8, Fachgruppe Informatik, RWTH Aachen, Germany.

[13] Maggiolo-Schettini, A. Peron, "A Graph Rewriting Framework for Statecharts Semantics", Proc. 5th Int. Workshop on Graph Grammars and their Application to Computer Science, 1996.

[14] Bredenfeld, R. Camposano, "Tool integration and construction using generated graph-based design representations", Proceedings of the 32nd ACM/IEEE conference on Design automation conference, p.94-99, June 12-16, 1995, San Francisco, CA.

[15] Object Management Group, Object Constraint Language Specification, OMG Document formal/01-9-77. September 2001.

[16] Karsai G.: Design Tool Integration: An Exercise in Semantic Interoperability, Proceedings of the IEEE Engineering of Computer Based Systems, Edinburgh, UK, March, 2000.

[17] Szemethy,T., Karsai,G,.: Platform Modeling and Model Transformations for Analysis, Vol 10. No. 10., pp 1383-1406, Journal of Universal Computer Science, 2004.

[18] Personal communication with engineers of a major US automotive manufacturer.

[19] Uwe Assmann, "Aspect Weaving by Graph Rewriting", Generative Component-based Software Engineering (GCSE), p. 24-36, Oct 1999.

[20] J. Gray, G. Karsai, "An Examination of DSLs for Concisely Representing Model Traversals and Transformations", 36th Annual Hawaii International Conference on System Sciences (HICSS'03) - Track 9, p. 325a, January 06 - 09, 2003.

[21] T. Clark, A. Evans, S. Kent, P. Sammut: "The MMF Approach to Engineering Object-Oriented Design Languages," Workshop on Language Descriptions, Tools and Applications (LDTA2001), April, 2001

[22] Keith Duddy: UML2 must enable a family of languages. CACM 45(11): 73-75 (2002).

[23] Whittle, J., Saboo, J. and Kwan, R. "From Scenarios to Code: An Air Traffic Control Case Study." Journal of Software and Systems Modeling, Vol 4(1), 2005, pp. 71-93.

[24] R. Mathew, I. H. Krüger: Component Synthesis from Service Specifications. In: Leue, Stefan; Systä, Tarja J. (Eds.): Scenarios: Models, Transformations and Tools International Workshop, Dagstuhl Castle, Germany, September 7-12, 2003, Revised Selected Papers, Lecture Notes in Computer Science, Vol. 3466, Springer 2005.

[25] Johannes Koskinen, Erkki Mäkinen, and Tarja Systä, Implementing a Component-Based Tool for Interactive Synthesis of UML Statechart Diagrams, an extended version of the SPLST 2001 paper, Acta Cybernetica, vol 15, number 4, 2002.

[26] T. Dang: "Verification and Synthesis of Hybrid Systems", Ph.D. thesis, INPG, 2000.

[27] Mitchell: "Application of Level Set Methods to Control and Reachability Problems in Continuous and Hybrid Systems", PhD Dissertation, Stanford University, 2002.

[28] R. Alur, R. Grosu, Y. Hur, V. Kumar, I. Lee, "Modular Specification of Hybrid Systems in CHARON." Proceedings of the 3rd International Workshop on Hybrid Systems: Computation and Control, Pittsburgh, PA, March 23-25, 2000.

[29] Agrawal,A., Simon, Gy., Karsai, G.: Semantic Translation of Simulink/Stateflow models to Hybrid Automata using Graph Transformations, Electronic Notes in Theoretical Computer Science,Volume 109, Pages 43-56, Proceedings of the Workshop on Graph Transformation and Visual Modeling Techniques (GT-VMT 2004) .

[30] Distributed Real-Time Systems: Monitoring, Debugging, and Visualization, (Y. Bi, S. Yang, and R. Smith), John Wiley & Sons, Inc., New York, 1996.

[31] Alexander Pretschner, Heiko Lotzbeyer, Jan Philipps. "Model Based Testing in Evolutionary Software Development," IWRSP, vol. 00, no. , p. 0155, 12th 2001.

[32] J. Greenfield, and K. Short: "Software Factories: Assembling Applications with Patterns, Models, Frameworks, and Tools ", John Wiley, 2004.

Software for Automotive Systems: Model-Integrated Computing

Sandeep Neema and Gabor Karsai

Institute for Software Integrated Systems, Vanderbilt University
2015 Terrace Place
Nashville, TN 37203
sandeep.neema@vanderbilt.edu

Abstract. Embedded Automotive systems are becoming increasingly complex, and as such difficult to design and develop. Model-based approaches are gaining foothold in this area, and increasingly the system design and development is being conducted with model-based tools, most notably Matlab® Simulink® and Stateflow® from Mathworks Inc., among others. However, these tools are addressing only a limited aspect of the system design. Moreover, there is a lack of integration between these tools, which makes overall system design and development cumbersome and error-prone. Motivated by these shortcomings we have developed an approach, based on Model-Integrated Computing, a technology matured over a decade of research at ISIS, Vanderbilt University. The centerpiece of this approach is a graphical modeling language, Embedded Control Systems Language for Distributed Processing (ECSL-DP). A suite of translators and tools have been developed that facilitate the integration of ECSL-DP with industry standard Simulink and Stateflow tools, and open the possibility for integration of other tools, by providing convenient and extensible interfaces. A code generator has been developed that synthesizes implementation code, configuration and firmware glue-code from models. The approach has been prototyped and evaluated with a medium scale example. The results demonstrate the promise of the approach, and points to interesting directions for further research.

1 Introduction

Embedded automotive systems are becoming notoriously difficult to design and develop. Over the past years there has been an explosion in the scale and complexity of these systems, owing to a push towards drive-by-wire technologies, increasing feature levels, and increasing capabilities in the embedded computing platforms. In order to address this level of complexity, the automotive industry has in general embraced the model-based design approach for embedded systems development, however the approach is confined to only the functional aspects of the system design and restricted to a limited suite of tools, most notably the Mathworks family of Matlab®, Simulink® (SL), Stateflow® (SF) tools. Undeniably Simulink and Stateflow are very powerful, graphical system design tools for modeling and simulating, continuous and discrete event-based behavior of a dynamical system. However, these tools by no means cover the entire gamut of embedded systems development. Functional design, howsoever

M. Broy, I.H. Krüger, and M. Meisinger (Eds.): ASWSD 2004, LNCS 4147, pp. 116–136, 2006.
© Springer-Verlag Berlin Heidelberg 2006

difficult, is only one aspect of embedded systems development. There are several other complex activities such as requirement specification, verification, mapping on to a distributed platform, scheduling, performance analysis, and synthesis, among others in the embedded systems development process. The bright side is that there are tools which individually support one or more of these other developmental activities. The down side is of course a lack of integration (or otherwise limited integration with proprietary interfaces) among these tools and the Mathworks family of tools, which makes it extremely difficult to maintain a consistent view of the system as the design progresses through the development process, and also requires significant manual efforts in creating different representations of the same system for different tools.

Motivated by this severe shortcoming we are developing an approach, based on Model-Integrated Computing (MIC) [1], a mature technology developed at Institute for Software Integrated Systems (ISIS), Vanderbilt University over a decade of research. The approach presented here is not designed to replace the individual tools in the development process, but complement these tools as an integrator, by facilitating interchange between the different tools, and providing convenient and open interfaces with which it is possible to integrate new tools with relatively modest effort. The key ingredient of our approach is an extensible graphical modeling language that we call Embedded Control Systems Language for Distributed Processing (ECSL-DP). We surround this language with a suite of translators and tools that facilitate the integration of this language in the embedded automotive developments process, starting from functional specification down to synthesis of executable code for the distributed platform.

The toolsuite was motivated by the following automotive example. Today, many functionalities in cars are implemented by a number of electronic control units (ECUs), often developed by a number of suppliers. The software for ECU-s is developed using the Simulink/Stateflow tools, often using the code generator available for those tools. However this development process focuses on a single ECU, not a network of CPU-s. When this project was performed the ECU developers did not have tools for generating code from Simulink/Stateflow models for a network of ECUs, nor for the end-to-end analysis of multi-ECU systems. On the other hand, models for existing ECU-s *were* available. The ECSL-DP toolchain provides a way for (1) reusing existing models, (2) generating code for multiple ECU-s running a (distributed) software platform, and (3) interfacing with model analysis tools (if they are available).

The rest of the paper is organized as follows: Section 2 provides an overview of the modeling language ECSL-DP. Section 3 describes the ECSL-DP code-generator. Section 4 describes a tool-chain built with ECSL-DP. Section 5 describes a small case study in the application of the tool chain to an automotive application. Section 6 provides an overview of related work. Section 7 concludes this paper and offers suggestions for future work.

2 Embedded Control Systems Language for Distributed Processing (ECSL-DP)

ECSL-DP is a graphical design modeling language supported by Graphical Modeling Environment (GME), a meta-programmable graphical modeling tool developed at

ISIS, Vanderbilt University [2]. For GME, a modeling language is defined in terms of meta-models that capture the abstract syntax, and static semantics of the language. It has concepts and constructs suited for modeling distributed automotive embedded applications. Once the language was defined, the GME meta-programming technology allowed the instantiation of a new graphical modeling environment, supporting the visual specification and editing of ECSL-DP models. GME uses an annotated UML class diagram for meta-modeling (i.e., to define a new modeling language). We utilize this definition of ECSL-DP here. The key categories of modeling concepts in ECSL-DP include:

1. Dataflow Modeling – for hierarchical dataflow-diagram oriented modeling of signal flows, representing the functional design.
2. Stateflow Modeling – for hierarchical state machine diagrams, representing finite-state behavior, in the functional design.
3. Component Modeling – for modeling of software components and partitioning of functional design over software components. Components are software artifacts that get instantiated on an embedded platform.
4. Hardware Topology Modeling – for modeling of the topology of the distributed platform including ECU-s, Buses, their physical ports, and their connectivity.
5. Deployment (Mapping) Modeling – for modeling of the deployment of components on ECU-s, including association with RTOS tasks, and mapping of component ports on to physical communication conduits (sensors, actuators, and bus messages)

Note that the dataflow and stateflow sub-languages are very similar to SL/SF. This is motivated by the need for integrating with the SL/SF tools, and we have developed translators that automatically derive this portion of ECSL-DP models from SL/SF models. Below, we describe these categories of modeling concepts with their respective meta-models.

2.1 Dataflow Modeling

This sub-language of ECSL-DP supports the dataflow-oriented modeling of dynamical systems (see Figure 1). The toplevel container for Dataflow models is a `System` which is a `<<Model>>` (in the GME terminology) contained in the `Simulink` folder. `Systems` are hierarchical as can be observed from the containment relation between the `System` class, and the `Block` class which is an abstract generalization of the `System` class. `Systems` are semantically equivalent to the SL concept of SubSystems, and the composition semantics are that of the dataflow model of computation [5]. Thus, a `System` class defines a dataflow relation between the contained `Blocks` (which may be `Systems`, `Primitives`, or `References`), using the `Line` association class, that associates `Ports` of `Blocks`. Note that `Blocks`, `Ports` and `Connectors` are abstract base types (i.e. they cannot be instantiated, thus there are no model elements directly corresponding to them). `Blocks` are subclassed into `Systems`, `References`, and `Primitives`. The `Reference` class represents an imported block (a library block in SL/SF), while a `Primitive` is a basic block, that has a concrete implementation, and it exists in the local context.

`Blocks` also contain `Parameters` and `Annotations`. `Parameters` define configurable properties of a block, for example, the *Gain* parameter of the *Gain* primitive, allows configuration of the gain factor with which the block amplifies the input. `Annotations` are documentation concept that allows a developer to annotate and insert textual comments in an essentially graphical specification. `Annotations` do not have any operational semantics.

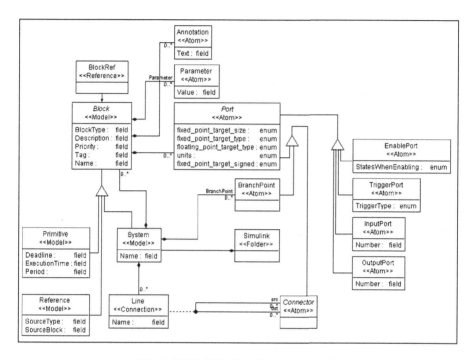

Fig. 1. ECSL-DP – Dataflow meta-model

`Ports` are subclassed into `EnablePorts`, `TriggerPorts`, `InputPorts`, and `OutputPorts`, each of which corresponds to equivalent modeling concepts in SL/SF and has the same semantics. `Connectors` are sub-classed into `Ports` and `BranchPoints`. The `Connector` abstraction is simply a meta-modeling convenience, which allows abstracting all entities that can participate in a dataflow association, specified with the `Line` association class. Notice that the association class `Line` is stereotyped as a `<<Connection>>` and implies a specific visualization as connecting lines in GME. Thus, `Lines` denote dataflows among `Blocks` within a `System` (via their `Ports` and intermediate `BranchPoints`).

2.2 Stateflow Modeling

The sub-language of the ECSL-DP supports the modeling of hierarchical parallel finite state machines, the semantics of which are described in [6] (see Figure 2). The `Stateflow` folder contains `State <<Model>>`s, which are root models for hierarchical state machines, and is equivalent to the State concept in SF. Each `State` can contain a number of `Data`, and `Event` objects – each of which has the same semantics as the equivalent concepts in SF, and subclasses of the (abstract) `Trans-Connector` (as in "transition" connector) class. The subclasses of `TransConnector` include `Junctions`, `TransInPorts`, `TransOutPorts`, `TransStart` (as in "transition" input and output ports and starting points), `History`, and `ConnectorRefs` (which are `<<Reference>>`s pointing to objects derived from the `TransConnector` base class). `States` contain `Transition` `<<Connection>>`s. These connections connect two objects (derived from the `TransConnector` class), and represent the state transition concepts of the hierarchical finite state machine. The operational semantics of transition is the same as those of transitions in SF; however, the graphical representation differs.

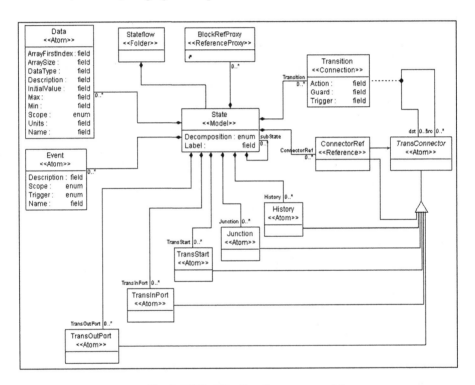

Fig. 2. ECSL-DP – Stateflow meta-model

A `State` model also contains a `BlockRef` `<<Reference>>`, which points to a `Block` (contained in a `System`, described above). This mechanism provides the linkage between a Stateflow model and a Simulink model. Within the Simulink hierarchy a state machine is represented as a `System` that has `Ports`. These `Ports` have the same name as the input and output `Data` variables in the state machine model. This `System` object contains a `Primitive` S-Function Block, which is referred in the `State`, thus denoting the correspondence.

2.3 Component Modeling

The Component modeling sub-language of ECSL-DP allows componentization of functional designs. Components are ported objects that encapsulate SL/SF Systems, and can be deployed on the platform as a unit. Component ports are associated with the ports of the encapsulated System, and capture concrete data-types used in inter-component communication.

Figure 3 shows the Component modeling portion of the ECSL-DP modeling language. A ComponentSheet<<Model>> is a container for Component <<Model>>-s, as well as for component interactions which are modeled with Signal<<Connection>>-s. For reasons of scalability, and avoiding visual clutter, ECSL-DP allows a designer to create multiple ComponentSheet models and distribute Components over these. When there is a need to model an interaction between Components that are not located on the same ComponentSheet, a designer must create a ComponentShortcut<<Reference>> in the Component-Sheet where he wants to make the connection. Component-s contain System-Ref<<Reference>>, which is a reference to a System<<Model>>. A CPort<<Atom>>-s, is an abstract class, concretized as CInPort<<Atom>>-s and COutPort<<Atom>>-s. These represent component ports and define the input and output interface of a component. A Signal<<Connection>> is an association class that represents connections between component ports. InPortMapping<<Connection>> and OutPortMapping<<Connection>> are association classes that represent mapping of System ports to component ports. An RTConstraint<<Atom>> allows capturing real-time constraints over component ports. The Latency attribute specifies the desired real-time constraint, over when an input is received on an associated CInPort (associated via RTCIn<<Connection>>), and when the output is generated on the corresponding COutPort (associated via RTCOut<<Connection>>).

2.4 Hardware Modeling

The hardware modeling sublanguage of ECSL-DP allows the designer to specify the hardware topology, including the processors and communication links between the processors. These models introduce new model types: ECU-s (which are processors hosting the components), buses (that establish the communication links between the processors, and thus the software components).

Figure 4 shows the Hardware Modeling portion of the ECSL-DP meta-model. A HardwareSheet<<Model>> represents the hardware topology that is composed with ECU-s, Buses, and inter-connects. It contains HWElement<<FCO>> which is sub-classed as ECU<<Model>>, Bus<<Atom>>, and BusConnector<<Connection>>. ECU-s contain Channel-s that represent the physical interface of an ECU. A Channel<<FCO>> is an abstract class, concretized as IChan<<Atom>>, OChan<<Atom>>, and BusChan<<Set>>. IChan-s represent sensor ports, OChan-s represent actuator ports, and BusChan-s represent bus connection ports. A FirmwareModule<<Atom>> represents a firmware driver

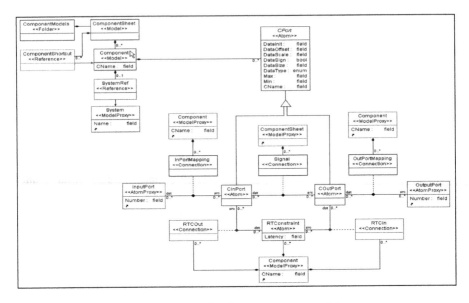

Fig. 3. ECSL-DP – Component meta-model

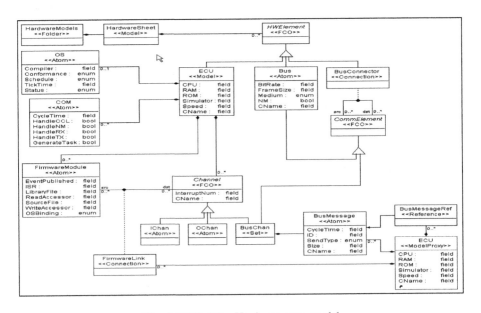

Fig. 4. ECSL-DP – Hardware meta-model

that can be attached to a `Channel` with the `FirmwareLink<<Connection>>`. A `BusConnector<<Connection>>` is an association class representing architectural connections between `Bus`, and `BusChan-s` of `ECU-s`. A `BusMessage<<Atom>>` represents a physical bus message, a basic unit of communication transported over a bus. `BusMessage`-s are associated with `BusChan`-s with the Set membership containment relation.

2.5 Deployment Modeling

The deployment models capture the *mapping* (or allocation) of software components onto the hardware architecture. The ECU model has a "deployment aspect" that allows the designer to capture SW component to ECU mapping using GME's reference concept. In this aspect of the ECU models, references ("pointers") can be placed that indicate that an instance of the component is allocated to the specific ECU. Note that deployment models are separate from software models, thus allowing the reuse of software models in different HW architectures. Furthermore, component ports are connected to ECU ports (sensor, actuators, and bus connections) to indicate how the component software interfaces map to actual sensors, actuators and buses.

Figure 5 shows the Mapping (deployment) modeling portion of the ECSL-DP metamodel. A `ComponentRef<<Reference>>` is a reference to a Component described earlier. `ComponentRef`-s can be contained in ECU-s to indicate the mapping of components. A `Task<<Set>>` represents an OS task, and the assignment of a `Component` to a task is expressed with the set membership containment relation. `InCommMapping<<Connection>>`, and `OutCommMapping<<Connection>>`, is an association class (`CPort` to/from `CommDst`), which represents mapping of component ports to hardware channels. Noticeably `CPort`s are not directly associated to a `BusChan`, but to a `BusMessage`. Multiple component ports can be multiplexed over a single `BusMessage`. A `BusMesssage` is a first-class entity in the underlying bus communication firmware.

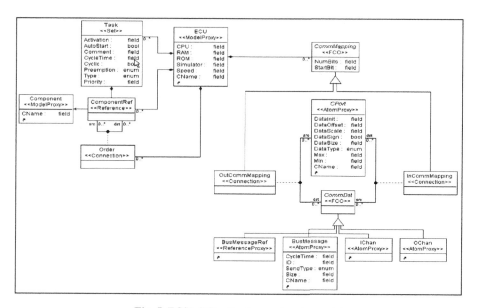

Fig. 5. ECSL-DP – Deployment meta-model

Mapping modeling relies on a GME visualization technique that allows for attaching multiple views (referred to as `Aspects` in GME terminology) to a model, and enabling selective visualization of different parts of a model. The ECU models have two aspects (not visible in the portion of the meta-model shown above): (1) Topology aspect, and (2) Mapping aspect. The topology aspect visualizes topological elements of the hardware platform, while the mapping aspect visualizes mapping elements.

3   ECSL-DP Code Generator

The code generator component synthesizes code artifacts necessary for system implementation. Figure 6 shows the artifacts that are generated by the ECSL-DP/CG. As can be seen in the figure, the following types of files are generated:

- **OSEK OIL-File:** For each ECU-node in the network an oil file is generated, that includes a listing of all used OSEK objects and their relations (see OSEK specification).
- **OSEK Tasks & Code:** All tasks are implemented in one or more C code files.
- **Application Behavior Code:** A separate function is generated for each application component that implements the behavior of the component. This function is called out from within a task frame.
- **Glue Code:** The glue code comprises one or more C code/header files that resolve the calls to the CAN driver or the firmware in order to provide access to CAN signals or HW I/O signals.

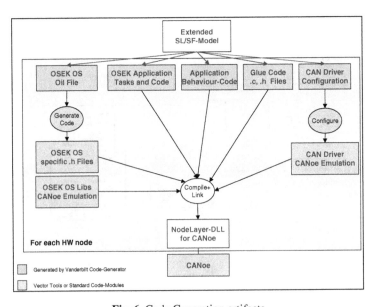

Fig. 6. Code Generation artifacts

The description of all code-generator components can be seen elsewhere [9], in the subsequent discussion we restrict attention to the Stateflow (sub-language of ECSL-DP) to C code generator, which is developed using GReaT, a graph rewriting tool developed at ISIS, Vanderbilt University [8]. The reason for focusing on this transformation is for demonstrating the use and potential of graph-rewriting techniques, which offers a cleaner, self-documenting, and formally analyzable approach to code-generation. In fact an extension to our approach generates test suites automatically from the code-generator specifications.

The output of the code generator is a C program that implements the logic of the state-machine. The generated C code is a stylized subset of C, an abstract machine, for which we have created a UML meta-model that we call SFC (see Fig. 7 below). Note that the SFC meta-model is an important contribution of this work, as it leads to a cleaner semantic underpinning of Stateflow by explicitly formulating the abstract machine, and the concepts and relationships within this abstract machine. The key entities in this meta-model are described below:

- SFFile – the top-level file object, container for the state-machine code
- InitFxn – initialization function that must be invoked to initialize the state-machine
- RootFxn – the main entry point of the state-machine
- SFData, SFEvent – the data, event variables within the state-machine. These variables form the input and output argument list of the root function, note the association between RootFxn and DE, the abstract base class of SFData and SFEvent
- Enter, Exit, Exec – these are the entry, exit, and step function corresponding to each compound state in the state-machine. Fxn is the abstract base class representing a function.
- SFState – these represent the states in the state machine, in the generated code these are represented with indexed labels in an enumeration list.
- ActiveSubStates – this singleton array variable represents the current list of active sub-state for each compound state in the state machine. The enumeration value of the compound state is used to index into this array to determine the current active sub-state in the generated code.
- Statement – this abstract base class represent code blocks in the generated code. Statements are sub-classed into CompoundStatements, and PrimitiveStatements. CompoundStatements are code blocks that include other Statements. These are sub-classed as Switch, Case, If, and Fxn. PrimitiveStatements are FxnCall, Break, Return, ArgComp, Activate, IsInactive, UExpr, etc.

Note that the graph transformation is a set of graph rewrite rules that produces an object graph compliant with the SFC meta-model. A secondary code-generator, which could be considered as an anti-parser, prints the C-code after traversing the SFC object graph. In the rest of this section we describe the transformation by showing

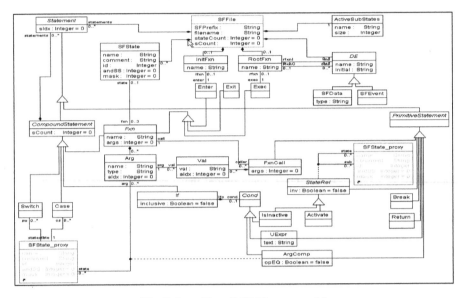

Fig. 7. State-Flow C (SFC) meta-model

screen-capture of key parts of the transformation specification. It should be noted here that the transformation language implemented by the GReaT tool, has a control flow structure in addition to the graph rewriting instructions. The details of the graph transformation language can be seen here[1] [8].

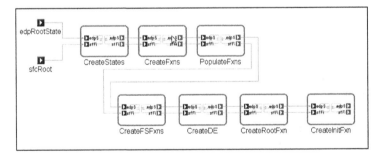

Fig. 8. Top-level ECSL-DP to SFC transformation rule

Figure 8 shows the top-level transformation rule. The top-level rule shows the sequencing of sub-rules. The boxes represent compound rules, and the port objects and their interconnections represent passing of objects to and from the rules. The ports `edpRootState`, and `sfcRoot` in the top-level rule are bound to the top-level state in the ECSL-DP network which is to be transformed, and the root object (a singleton

---

[1] The modeling environment uses a color scheme to highlight certain syntactic constructs. In the text we refer to this coloring, which would be visible in a color printout of the figures.

instance of SFFile) in the SFC data-network, respectively. There are seven key steps in the transformation, as shown by the seven sub-rules in the top level rule. The CreateStates rule creates SFState objects in the output data network, whereas the CreateFxns object creates Enter, Exit, and Exec functions. The PopulateFxns rule populates these functions. We navigate down into this rule next.

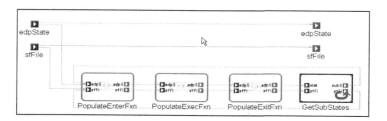

Fig. 9. PopulateFxn rule in the ECSL-DP to SFC transformation

Figure 9 shows the PopulateFxn rule. There are three sub-rules in this rule corresponding to the population of Enter, Exit, and Exec function. The fourth rule GetSubStates is visualized differently from the other rules as it is a proxy to a rule defined elsewhere, and demonstrate the ability to reuse rules. Also note the arrows going the GetSubStates rule back to the PopulateEnterFxn rule. This represents a form of recursion - GetSubState rule returns the sub-states of the current state, and the other rules are invoked on the sub-states.

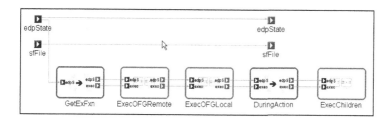

Fig. 10. PopulateExecFxn Rule in the ECSL-DP to SFC transformation

Figure 10 shows the PopulateExecFxn rule. This rule generates code for the Exec fuction, which implements a step in a state-machine. The generated code for the step function must check for enabled transitions leading out of this state, and if there is an enabled transition then the transition must be taken which requires a call to the exit function of the source state, performing the transition actions, and invoking the enter function of the destination state in the simplest case. If no transitions are enabled then the during action of the state must be performed, and then the step function must do a step on the sub-states. The ExecOFGRemote, and the ExecOFGLocal sub-rules of this rule emit the code for checking for enabled transitions and performing the transition step. The ExecOFGRemote rule handles remote transitions (source and destination state have different parents), while the ExecOFGLocal rule handles local transitions (source and destination state have the same parent). The ExecOF-GRemote rule is invoked prior to the ExecOFGLocal rule since cross-hierarchy transitions have a higher priority than local transitions. The DuringAction is a primitive rule (denoted with red-colored border in the graphical tool), and we examine it next.

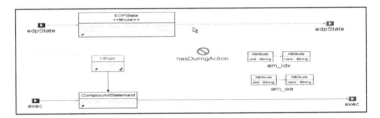

Fig. 11. DuringAction Rule in the ECSL-DP to SFC transformation

Figure 11 shows the DuringAction rule. This is a graph rewrite rule, which typically consist of a LHS which represents a pattern to be matched, and RHS which represents the modification in the graph. In this particular rule the pattern is simply an ECSL-DP State, and a CompoundStatement, which are objects passed as input to this rule. The class UExpr represents creation (denoted with a blue border in the graphical modeling tool) of a new object instance of the UExpr class. Also, the composition arrow represents creation (also denoted with a blue line) of a composition relation between the CompoundStatement object and the created UExpr statement. In simple words this rule creates a UExpr object in the output data-network. The boxes labeled am_idx, and am_ea contain attribute mapping specifications. These are code snippets which are executed by the transformation engine when the pattern is matched. The circle labeled hasDuringAction is a guard which must be satisfied for the pattern to be matched. In this particular case the guard simply checks that the State has a during action.

There are ~75 rules in this transformation specification; clearly a description of all the rules is outside the scope of this paper. The transformation rules and the SFC meta-model together capture the operational semantics of Stateflow. The GReaT engine, compiles these transformation specification into compilable C++ code. The code is compiled and linked with the other code generation stages to build the complete ECSL-DP CG, which when executed on the input model produces all the code-artifacts listed earlier.

4 ECSL-DP Tool-Chain

As stated earlier in the introduction, our key motivation is to provide an integrated tool-chain that addresses several aspects of distributed automotive embedded systems design in an integrated manner. Figure 12 shows the prototype tool-chain that we have setup, and the information flow through this tool-chain. In this integrated tool-chain the initial functional design, and simulation takes place in the industry standard SL/SF tools. In a related research project we have also developed, an Automated Model Compiler (AMC) tool [10], that given an abstract architectural design consisting of SL models of subsystems, and alternatives, composes the functional design automatically, after trading-off design choices and satisfying a user-defined set of constraints. The outcome of the AMC tool is a SL model that captures the functional design for the automotive system. We have also developed a UML meta-model for SL/SF [11], and using the UDM tool [7] we have been able to provide automatically generated API-s that makes the SL/SF data openly accessible, and manipulable. Utilizing this API we developed a translator that transforms SL/SF model into equivalent functional design models in ECSL-DP. The software componentization of the functional design, the platform design, and the specification of deployment then proceeds in the GME/ECSL-DP modeling environment. Currently all the partitioning is done manually, however we plan to develop utility packages that help a system designer in performing this step in an automated/semi-automated manner. The UDM tool is again used to generate API-s that facilitates integration of 3rd party tools with GME/ECSL-DP. To demonstrate this integration we have developed translators utilizing this API to generate inputs for a suite of analysis tools, including Giotto that can perform a variety of timing analysis on the models. The results of the analysis can be fed back into the ECSL-DP, and the design re-iterated to arrive at a feasible design. The ECSL-DP Code generators then produce all the necessary artifacts for instantiating the design on a platform. It is also possible to integrate 3rd party code-generators with ECSL-DP and utilize their capabilities. The correctness of code-generator is often a key concern for the automotive engineers, and as mentioned earlier we are developing a code-generator testing technique in collaboration with Daimler-Chrysler engineers, that is integrated in this tool-chain and helps with validation of the code-generator itself.

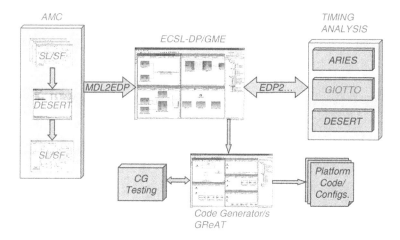

Fig. 12. ECSL-DP tool-chain

The tool-chain as shown in this figure is deployed on an Open Tool-Integration Framework (OTIF) [12] that facilitates provision and automated execution of a workflow setup using the tools in the tool-chain. The OTIF tool uses CORBA as the underlying distribution service which facilitates setting up the workflow in a fully distributed setting with multiple engineers, and multiple workstations, which is critical in a large enterprise with multiple teams working on different aspects of an automotive system design.

This tool-chain, and tools and translators, reported in this paper are publicly available through the ESCHER repository, a joint industry-government sponsored consortium [13].

5   Case Study: Rear Window Defroster

This section presents a case study in the application of the ECSL-DP tool chain. A Rear Window Defroster (RWD) was chosen as it is a distributed embedded automotive system sufficiently complex to exercise various capabilities of the tool-suite, and yet manageable enough to be presentable in a short discourse on the use of the tools. We first give a short overview of the example, and then describe steps through the design flow.

5.1   RWD Overview

The RWD system is responsible for defrosting the rear window of an automobile. In addition to the defrosting control, the system is also responsible for updating a display indicating the status, and monitoring the battery voltage levels. The controller processes the temperature sensors information, and generates actuation signals for the heater unit. The RWD system is implemented on multiple ECU-s, since the actuators and sensors are shared by other systems within the automobile.

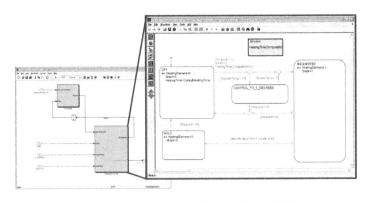

Fig. 13. Top-level Simulink Model of RWD

5.2 RWD Functional Design

The functional design of the RWD system was conducted by DaimlerChrysler engineers using the SL/SF tools. The two main functions of the RWD system (as captured in this case study) are to provide a Defrost controller, and a Display controller. Figure 13 shows a screen capture of the top-level SL model, elaborating the SF model of the Defrost Controller subsystem. This SL/SF model was imported into ECSL-DP using the MDL2EDP utilities and was used to populate the Dataflow/Stateflow modeling portions of the overall system model. The rest of the system modeling and design was conducted in the GME/ECSL-DP environment.

5.3 RWD Component Design

Figure 14 shows the component design of the RWD system, conducted in the GME/ECSL-DP environment, which shows the components and their interactions. Two components can be seen, each of which correspond to a controller of the RWD system listed earlier. Note that the view shown in Figure 14 is that of a Component-Sheet<<Model>> (refer to the ECSL-DP Component meta-model), and the Components (grey-boxes) are instances of Component<<Model>>-s. The port graphics on the boxes represent the CInPort<<Atom>> and COutPort<<Atom>> objects contained in Component<<Model>>-s.

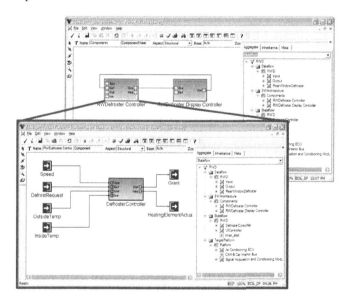

Fig. 14. Component design model of RWD in ECSL-DP

While performing the component design an automotive engineer is expected to supply concrete data-typing information as attributes of the CInPort and COutPort. Figure 14 also shows the "drill-down" into the RWDefrosterController component. The component contains a reference to the DefrosterController System from the functional design. The input and output ports of the System are mapped to the CInPort and COutPort of the Component as depicted with the connections in the figure. The mapping also includes the specifics of concrete data-typing, including scaling and offsets.

5.4 RWD Platform Design

In parallel with the SW component design, the HW platform design is performed. This involves modeling the ECU-s, Bus-s, Sensor-s, Actuator-s, Bus port-s of ECU-s and interconnects. Figure 15 shows the platform model of the RWD system, with two ECU-s and a CAN Bus. The ECU-s are connected to the Bus with BusConnector<<Connection>> between BusChan ports of ECU-s. The platform design also involves setting the attributes of the ECU-s dealing with processor speed, available memory, and defining the specifics of the OS. Bus Messages are also defined as part of this exercise, and the attributes of the Bus Messages are configured to define the size of the message, its priority, and the frequency of its transmission over the bus. Additional attributes related to communication over the bus are defined as the attributes of the COM object.

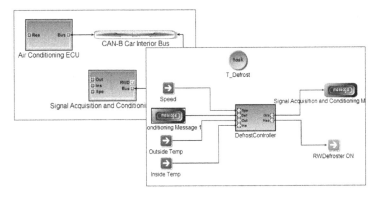

Fig. 15. RWD Platform Design and Component Mapping Models

5.5 RWD Component Mapping

The final modeling step involves mapping the SW Components over ECU-s. The mapping also defines the OS Task binding of components, and mapping of component ports to Sensor-s/Actuator-s and Bus messages. Figure 15 shows a mapping view of one of the ECU-s. The shown ECU has the DefrostController Component mapped onto it. The component ports are connected to Sensor/Actuator ports or Bus messages. Two BusMessages can be seen, however, only one 'Signal Acquisition and Conditioning Module Message 1' is local to this ECU, the other messages is a references to Bus Messages from other ECU-s. One OS Tasks can also be observed in the figure. The association of tasks to Components is expressed with set membership relation, which is viewable in the Set mode of the GME editor.

5.6 RWD Generated Code

Subsequent to the completion of the modeling step, code generation is performed using the ECSL-DP/CG. This results in creation of several modeling artifacts as described earlier. The code generator creates a separate directory for each ECU, and produces the generated OIL files, and task, and firmware glue code in those directories. The label KLA below corresponds to the Air Conditioning ECU, and the label SAM_H corresponds to the Signal Acquisition and Conditioning Module. A single directory labeled System is also generated, which contains the generated behavior implementation code for individual components. The following table lists the generated files for the RWD example (the top-level directory containing the model is represented with $):

Table 1. Generated code from models

Directory	Files
$	HHS.dbc
$/KLA	KLA.oil, main.c, sigdefs.h, T_HBT_proc.c
$/SAM_H	SAM_H.oil, main.c, sigdefs.h, T_Fwd_proc.c, T_HST_proc.c
$/Systems	HHS_BA.c, HHS_BA_sl.c, HHS_ST.c, HHS_ST_sl.c, LokSpgFehlerErkennung_sl.c, Spannungs_berwachung.c

5.7 Deployment of Generated System on an Emulation Platform

The generated files listed above include functional code as well as configuration code. These files are processed and compiled by a suite of platform tools. We are using CANoe tools from Vektor-Informatik®. These include the CANdb tool for processing the communication matrix and generating the platform code for bus communication, the OIL compiler for processing the OIL file for each ECU and generating the task startup and platform configuration code, and the MSVC compiler for compiling the functional and the configuration code generated by the CANdb and OIL tools. The compilation results in a collection of DLL-s, which can be loaded by the CANoe Simulator for deploying, and executing the target system. The CANoe simulator allows configuring and generating test signals that emulates the sensors and environment. The simulator has a graphical front-end which allows monitoring and visualizing the sensor and actuator signals. Figure 16 shows a trace of two signals: a) user input to turn the defroster on or off, and b) the output of the controller to the heating actuator. The result of this and other tests that we conducted conform to the results obtained by simulating the system directly in Mathworks Simulink/Stateflow. We realize that this is not a formal validation of the correctness of the generators that we have developed; however, it does provide a degree of assurance in the correctness of generators.

The case study briefly presented here exercises the different elements of the toolchain: functional modeling, system modeling, and synthesis. The chosen case study, however, does not elicit strong analysis results particularly since it was an underconstrained system, which was trivially schedulable and allocable.

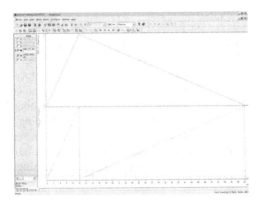

Fig. 16. Simulation output in the CANoe Tool from Vektor Informatik

6 Related Approaches

The work described in this paper is related to many approaches developed in the research community and industry. These connections are briefly summarized here.

The metamodeling approach is based on the use of a (stylized) UML, which is somewhat different from the MOF-based metamodeling promoted by OMG [14]. We believe our approach is more restrictive, but is still very flexible as illustrated by the success of our metaprogrammable modeling environment GME.

The ECSL-DP modeling language itself borrows a number of techniques from Simulink/Stateflow, but extends those with new concepts relevant for allocation, etc. In this respect it is similar to the approaches used in another domain-specific modeling language: ESML [15] which was used for modeling avionics architectures.

The tool integration framework has similar concepts as the "ModelBus" technique developed by a European research project [16], although the use of metamodeling and transformations is done in a somewhat different manner.

The technique and tool we used for implementing the code generator is related to graph transformation-based tools, like PROGRES [17], AGG [18], VIATRA [19], Fujaba [20]. It is distinguished by the use of explicit sequencing an dataflow semantics of rules.

The code generation approach is related to approaches used to generate code from dataflow graphs and StateChart diagrams, but is a unique implementation tailored for our needs.

Finally, the DaVinci tools from Vektor-Informatik [21] has similar elements of system modeling as ECSL-DP, however the significant difference is in the intrusive linkage to functional models developed in SL/SF. The DaVinci tools require that while developing functional models in SL/SF developers use blocks from a library provided by them. This affects the portability of the functional models locking them into a particular platform and tool. In ECSL-DP we create the link from functional models into component models externally, without explicitly modifying the functional design models in SL/SF.

7 Conclusions and Future Work

This report described a prototype Model-Integrated Computing based approach for development of Software for Automotive Systems, centered around a modeling language that we call "Embedded Control Systems Language for Distributed Processing" or ECSL-DP. We illustrate with this prototype, development of tool-chains that integrates industry standard tool-suite, and provides open interfaces for introducing other tools. We consider the ECSL-DP modeling language, and the Stateflow to C code generator a valuable contribution of this research.

We realize that the embedded systems development process is a large and vastly complicated one, and given the limited duration of this research it was not feasible to either cover the entire gamut, or even accomplish great depth in any one of the areas. As such there are several limitations in the prototyped approach that could be addressed with future research.

Some possible suggestions for future work in this area include enhancing the aspects of the modeling language, providing a deeper formal foundation for sub-languages of the ECSL-DP. We would also like to integrate hybrid systems analysis tools such as HSIF, Checkmate, and SAL, into the tool-chains.

Acknowledgements

The authors acknowledge the generous sponsorship of DARPA/IXO under the Model-based Integration of Embedded Systems project under which the core tools were developed. The authors also acknowledge Daimler Chrysler for its sponsorship and support in developing ECSL-DP and providing an example for evaluating the tools.

References

[1] Karsai G., Sztipanovits J., Ledeczi A., Bapty T.: Model-Integrated Development of Embedded Software, Proceedings of the IEEE, Vol. 91, Number 1, pp. 145-164, January, 2003.

[2] Generic Modeling Environment: a metaprogrammable modeling environment. For details see: http://www.isis.vanderbilt.edu/projects/GME/ The downloadable package includes detailed documentation and tutorial for modeling and metamodeling in GME.

[3] Mathworks web-site – http://www.mathworks.com

[4] Model-based Synthesis of Generators – http://www.isis.vanderbilt.edu/projects/MoBIES

[5] Lee, E. A. and Messerschmidt, D. G., "Static scheduling of synchronous data flow programs for digital signal processing," Transactions on Computers, C36 (1):24 --35, January 1987.

[6] Harel, D., "StateCharts: A visual Formalism for Complex Systems", Science of Computer Programming 8, pp 231-278, 1987.

[7] Magyari E., Bakay A., Lang A., Paka T., Vizhanyo A., Agrawal A., Karsai G.: UDM: An Infrastructure for Implementing Domain-Specific Modeling Languages, The 3rd OOPSLA Workshop on Domain-Specific Modeling, OOPSLA 2003, Anahiem, California, October 26, 2003.

[8] Agrawal A., Karsai G., Ledeczi A.: "An End-to-End Domain-Driven Software Development Framework", Domain-Driven Development track, 18th Annual ACM SIGPLAN Conference on Object-Oriented Programming, Systems, Languages, and Applications (OOPSLA), Anaheim, California, October 26, 2003.

[9] S. Neema and G. Karsai, "Embedded Control Systems Language for Distributed Processing," ISIS Technical Report, 2004.

[10] Neema S., Sztipanovits J., Karsai G., and Butts K., "Constraint-based Design-Space Exploration and Model Synthesis," Proceedings of Embedded Software Conference (EMSOFT), 2003, in Lecture Notes in Computer Science (LNCS), Springer-Verlag 2003.

[11] Neema S., "Analysis of Matlab Simulink and Stateflow Data Model," Technical Report, ISIS-01-204, March 2001.

[12] S. Neema G. Karsai, A. Lang., "Tool integration patterns," in Proceedings of Workshop on Tool Integration in System Development, European Software Engineering Conference, pages 33-38, 2003.

[13] ESCHER Web-site http://escher.isis.vanderbilt.edu

[14] Meta Object Facility http://www.omg.org/technology/documents/formal/mof.htm

[15] G. Karsai, S. Neema, B. Abbott, and D. Sharp, "A Modeling Languageand Its Supporting Tools for Avionics Systems," in Proceedings of 21st Digital Avionics Systems Conf., Aug. 2002.

[16] X. Blanc, "ModelBus: A ModelWare White Paper," http://www.modelware-ist.org/public_documents/ModelBusWhitePaper_MDDI.pdf

[17] A. Schurr. PROGRES: A Visual Language and Environment for PROgramming with Graph REwrite Systems. Aachener Informatik Bericht 94-11, RWTH Aachen, Fachgruppe Informatik, 1994.

[18] Manfred Nagl, Andy Schürr, Manfred Münch (Eds.): Applications of Graph Transformations with Industrial Relevance, International Workshop, AGTIVE'99, Kerkrade, The Netherlands, September 1-3, 1999, Proceedings. Lecture Notes in Computer Science 1779 Springer 2000, ISBN 3-540-67658-9

[19] D. Varr´o and G. Varr´o and A. Pataricza, Designing the Automatic Transformation of Visual Languages, volume 44, Elsevier, pages 205–227, Science of Computer Programming, 2002.

[20] U. Nickel and J. Niere and A. Z¨undorf, "Tool demonstration: The FUJABA environment", Proc. ICSE: The 22nd International Conference on Software Engineering, Limerick, Ireland, ACM Press, 200.

[21] http://www.vector-informatik.com/english/index.html?../products?davinci.html

Simulink Integration of Giotto/TDL

Wolfgang Pree, Gerald Stieglbauer, and Josef Templ

Software Research Group, Department of Computer Science
University of Salzburg, A-5020 Salzburg, Austria
{pree, stieglbauer, templ}@SoftwareResearch.Net

Abstract. The paper first presents the integration options of what we call the Timing Description Language (TDL) with MathWorks' Matlab/Simulink tools. Based on the paradigm of logical execution time (LET) as introduced by Giotto [2], TDL enhances Giotto towards a component architecture for real-time control applications [9]. The challenge is to provide appropriate visual and interactive modeling capabilities so that the developer can come up with the TDL timing model in the context of Simulink which has established itself as defacto modeling standard for control applications. The paper illustrates by means of a simple case study how we envision an adequate integration of both the TDL and the Simulink modeling approaches.

1 The Power of an Appropriate Software Model

Traditionally, control theory and hardware-based engineering have addressed the design of robust control applications using continuous-time signals. The permanent increase of the computing power of microprocessors has been reinforcing the trend to implement control functionality in software [3]. Software processes however, evolve in discontinuous time [4]. The distinction between embedded hardware and software systems lies conceptually in the different treatment of concurrency and the role of time [6]. As the complexity of embedded control applications increases, it is essential to introduce means to master the complexity of the software [5] and to define adequate methods and tools for building such control systems.

The buzz word model-based development has been coined to express that control and software engineers should use methods and tools that support application-centric development instead of a platform-centric approach. The key challenge is to identify the appropriate modeling abstractions and to provide a set of tools that better supports the process of modeling control applications. Giotto and its successor TDL illustrate the key ingredients of a good software model for control applications:

Application-Centric Abstractions. Traditionally, a control system is designed using tools for mathematical modeling and simulation, such as MathWorks' Simulink. Giotto has introduced the separation of the timing behavior from the functionality code (control laws). Giotto focuses only on the timing behavior. The functionality code can be programmed in any non-embedded programming language such as C. Simulink can be used to model the control laws and to generate the corresponding C code from these models.

M. Broy, I.H. Krüger, and M. Meisinger (Eds.): ASWSD 2004, LNCS 4147, pp. 137–154, 2006.

The main abstractions introduced by Giotto are the task and mode constructs. A task periodically computes a function (typically a control law). A mode contains a set of activities, task invocations, actuator updates and mode switches. A Giotto program is in one mode at a time. Mode switch conditions are checked periodically to determine whether to switch from the current mode to another one.

Tasks form the units of computation. They are invoked periodically with a specified frequency. They deliver results through task output ports connected to actuators or to other tasks, and they read input values from sensor ports or from output ports of other tasks. Thus, a TDL model specifies the real-time interaction of a set of components with the physical world, as well as the real-time interaction between the components.

What makes Giotto a good software model is the fact that the developer does not have to worry about platform details, for example: will the application be executed on a single node or on a distributed platform; which scheduling scheme ensures the timing behavior [4]; which device drivers copy the values from sensors or to actuators. Thus, the software model emphasizes application-centric transparency (simplicity), improves reliability and enables reuse, whereas the compiler that generates the code from the model emphasizes performance.

Determinism. The key property of the TDL semantics is the *logical execution time* (LET) assumption, which means that the execution times associated with all computation and communication activities are fixed and determined by the model, not by the platform. In TDL, the logical execution time of a task is always exactly the period of the task, and the logical execution times of all other activities (mode switching, data transfer across links, etc.) are always zero. According to [2] the LET assumption has all concurrent task executions within a TDL mode run logically in parallel. The logical execution time of a task is an abstract notion which is possibly very different from the actual, physical execution time of the task on a particular CPU, which may vary from task invocation to task invocation. The power of the LET assumption stems from the fact that logical, not physical execution times determine when sensors are read, when actuators are written, and when data travels across links.

As a consequence of the LET assumption, a TDL model is *environment determined*: for any given behavior of the physical world seen through the sensors, the model computes a *unique* trace of actuator values at periodic time instants [2]. In other words, the only source of nondeterminism in a TDL system is the physical environment. Furthermore, TDL represents a real-time process model that lifts program composition to process composition [10]: processes composed in that model compute, given a sequence of inputs, the same sequence of outputs (*value-determinism*) at the same time (*time-determinism*) provided the composition preserves the process timing (*time-invariant*) and is schedulable (*time-safe*), and the individual processes are value- and time-deterministic.

Syntax. The original syntax of both, Giotto and TDL is a textual one. The TDL language report [8] describes this representation of TDL programs in detail. Though one might prefer the textual representation of a TDL program, it was a goal from the beginning to also provide a visual and interactive modeling support for TDL. We aim at a seamless integration with the Simulink paradigm and tools, in particular its simulation capabilities. The paper first sketches the integration options of TDL and Simulink that have seemed to be the natural choices but finally turned out to lead to dead ends. Based on that experience we present in section 3 what we regard as the most suitable integration. The paper assumes that the reader has a basic knowledge about Mathworks' Matlab/Simulink tools.

2 TDL as Part of Simulink

This section describes what have seemed to be the two straight-forward integration approaches. We explain, why these integration approaches that we have actually implemented, have lead to a dead end. On the one hand this explains why we regard the third way, using Simulink as a back-end (section 3), as the most suitable one. On the other hand this might help to select the appropriate integration with Simulink for other model-based approaches.

2.1 TDL Tasks as Simulink S-Function Blocks

A Simulink model is composed of blocks and signal lines. Blocks contain either functionality which is used to calculate the output value(s) from the input value(s) of a block, or they contain further Simulink blocks. These container blocks are called Subsystem blocks and allow an arbitrary nesting. Subsystem blocks are the only means for structuring a Simulink model. From a programming language perspective, a Subsystem block corresponds conceptually to a function. Thus, the module construct is completely missing in Simulink. In other words, the Simulink modeling paradigm is stuck at function-oriented, top-down design. No module or class constructs which are nowadays regarded as essential for component-based development, are available for modeling.

Signal lines connect output ports of blocks with input ports of other ports and represent visually the data flow in a Simulink model. The common way of extending the Simulink functionality is through so-called System-function blocks (S-function blocks). Their functionality is programmed either in C, Ada, Fortran or Matlab. The program providing the particular S-function block behavior has to adhere to Simulink's callback architecture. This means that several callback functions have to be implemented in the chosen programming language. The most important callback functions are `mdlOutputs(...)` and `mdlUpdate(...)`. The execution phase of each Simulink block is an iterative computation of (1) the block outputs (2) block states and (3) the next time step. The function `mdlOutputs(...)` calculates the output of the block, while `mdlUpdate(...)` updates the block states.

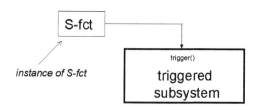

Fig. 1. A triggered Subsystem block in Simulink

The basic idea of coming up with a periodic task is to harness the subsystem triggering mechanism. Figure 1 illustrates this Simulink feature. If the triggering S-function block sends a 1 (true) via the data flow link to the subsystem, the subsystem is activated. Thus, the S-function block has to trigger the subsystem which represents a TDL task according to the desired frequency.

Managing a LET-based task communication requires that the result of a task execution (output values calculated by the Subsystem block) is communicated to another task after a fixed time period. Thus we need conceptually another S-function block that delays the communication of the values that flow between TDL tasks. To streamline the usage we have implemented the communication and triggering behavior described above in one S-function block. Figure 2 shows how a simple TDL program is specified with that S-function block. The S-function block has a clock as symbol inside. Note that one S-function block instance is used for triggering a subsystem and another one is used for the output signal line. The two Giotto tasks represented as Simulink subsystems simply increase their input by one. Task1 (upper Subsystem block in Figure 1) runs twice as fast as Task2.

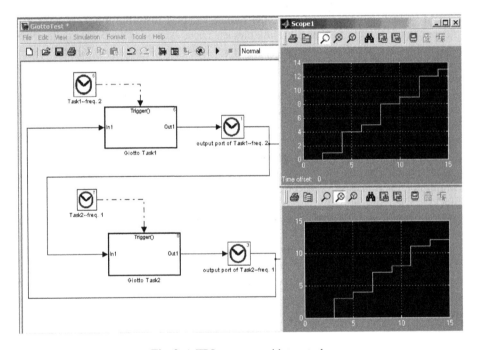

Fig. 2. A TDL program with two tasks

Benefits and drawbacks. The presented approach is the recommended choice for extending Simulink. Nevertheless, applying S-functions to TDL tasks is too fine-grained: The generated code (Real-Time Workshop) does not allow the preemption of TDL tasks.

This limitation is a show stopper: First, the time intervals between two simulation steps have to be as small as determined by the fastest TDL task. Second, all task computations have to be done within that interval. Thus, the S-Function integration option at the granularity of TDL tasks results in inefficient code that might be useless in practice in most situations.

Instead, the usage of S-functions to implement the TDL E-machine proved to be the ideal way of integrating TDL with Simulink. Section 3 sketches this usage of S-functions.

2.2 Integration of TDL Tasks and Modes Through Model Transformation

The basic idea of this kind of integration is to use standard Simulink blocks to model the LET behavior of TDL tasks. The Zero-Order-Hold (ZOH) and Unit-Delay (UD) blocks allow the modeling of this core TDL property. Figure 3 shows the TDL program with the same semantics as the one in Figure 2.

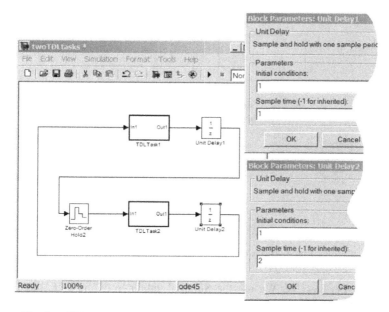

Fig. 3. A TDL program with two tasks constrained by ZOH and UD blocks

From the developer's point of view the insertion of the ZOH and UD blocks becomes inconvenient for more complex programs. With several tasks and numerous input and output lines it is tedious to place the ZOH and UD blocks and to define their parameters so that they correspond to the desired task periods. Above all, this would only suffice for simulation. To benefit from TDL, the compilable textual TDL program would have to be written by hand after the model simulation leads to satisfying results. This is why we have defined a TDL task block that is used to specify the model. The model then can be transformed by the S/TDL translator tool for simulation (the ZOH and UD blocks are inserted automatically by the S/TDL translator).

The S/TDL translator also generates the TDL textual program from the model. That can be compiled for a specific execution platform. Below we model a simple throttle control system to illustrate this approach. This sample application only comprises TDL tasks in one mode. So no modes and no mode switches have to be modeled.

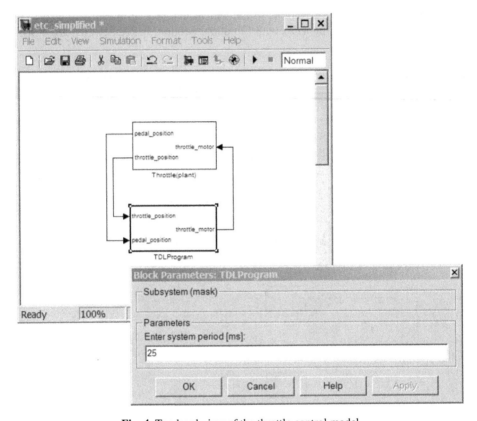

Fig. 4. Top level view of the throttle control model

Developer's Perspective. We use the Simulink editor to define both, the TDL program (timing aspects) and the functionality (control laws corresponding to the task functions) of the throttle controller. On the top level subsystem, we define the TDL controller and the plant, that is, the model of the throttle, which interacts with the controller during the simulation. To model the plant, we use standard Simulink blocks and put them into a subsystem block. To define the TDL controller, we use the so-called TDL program block from a library. Figure 4 shows the top level view of the model.

A TDL program block contains TDL task blocks, which are also in the TDL library. In our case study, only one task is needed for controlling the throttle (see Figure 5). In a dialog box the developer defines the task frequency relative to the period of the TDL program block and its initial output values. The initial output values are set to 0, while we configure the relative task frequency to 1, which means a task execution period of 25ms (hyper period defined for the TDL program block).

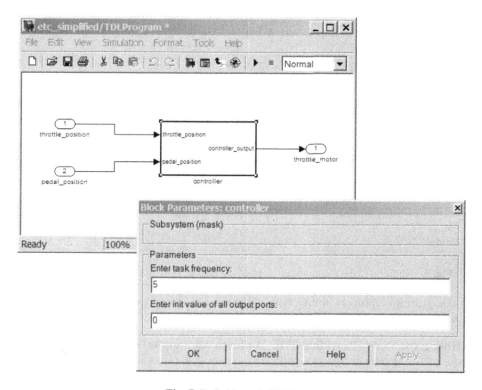

Fig. 5. Definition of a TDL task

Finally, we model the functionality of the task inside that subsystem block with the appropriate Simulink blocks (see Figure 6).

Simulation of a TDL Program. After modeling the controller in Simulink, the developer typically simulates it. For that purpose, the S/TDL translator tool translates the model to one which has the ZOH and UD blocks inserted so that the model exhibits the TDL semantics.

The translation results in a new Simulink model file. The developer loads that model into Simulink and starts the simulation. The user analyses the simulation results and decides if modifications have to be done to the original model. In this case, the developer changes the original model, repeats the translation step and starts the simulation again.

Code Generation. Once the model exhibits the desired behavior the code for the target platform has to be generated. We refrain from describing the details of the code generation process and refer the interested reader to [7]. The S/TDL translator generates on the one hand the textual TDL program which is then compiled with the TDL compiler. On the other hand glue code is generated that allows the linking of the TDL executable (timing code) with the functionality code, which is the C code generated from the tasks by means of one of the Simulink_to_C generator tools such as the Real-Time Workshop (RTW) or TargetLink. We have shown the feasibility of that

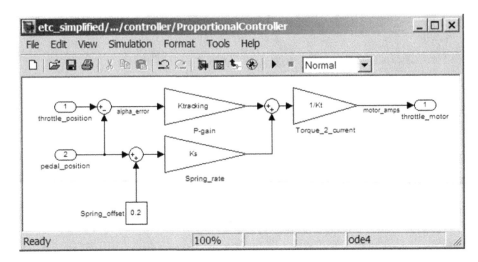

Fig. 6. Definition of the functionality (control law) of the TDL task that controls the throttle

code generation process in the realm of the throttle control example for the MPC555 platform, with the OSEK operating system and the RTW.

Hitting the Wall—Providing TDL Modes in Addition to TDL tasks. The semantics of TDL modes implies a significant increase in the complexity of the transformed model. As TDL mode switches correspond to constrained state transitions in state flow diagrams, the idea was to use Simulink's StateFlow editor for specifying a TDL mode switch. (The TDL mode switches are so far constrained as the mode switch

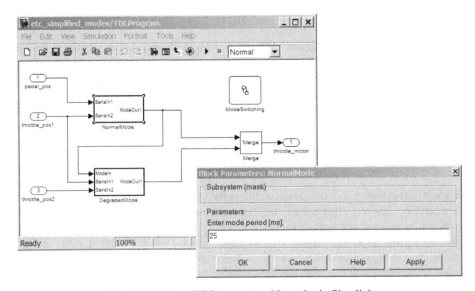

Fig. 7. Modeling a TDL program with modes in Simulink

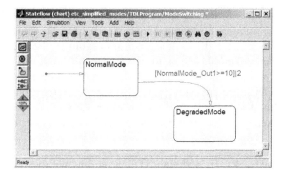

Fig. 8. Modeling mode switch conditions with the StateFlow editor

conditions are checked periodically, thus complying with the LET assumption. Furthermore TDL currently does not support nested modes.) Figures 7 and 8 show a sample model with two modes. The modes are modeled in the Simulink editor (Figure 7). We do not explain here the nasty detail that a merge block is required. The chart block represents a link to another editor, the StateFlow editor that is part of the Simulink tool suite. Figure 8 shows the modeling of the transition between the two modes in the StateFlow editor. Note that the variables used in the switch conditions, such as

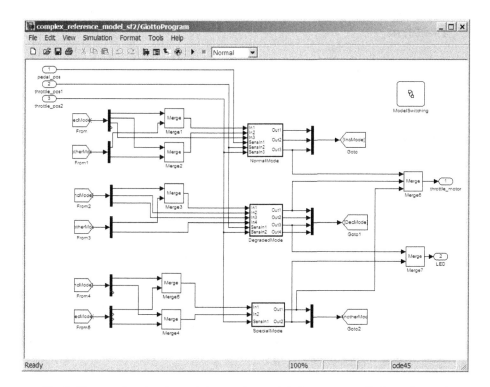

Fig. 9. Three modes already result in complex models that cannot easily be understood

NormalMode_out1 have to adhere to a naming convention so that the two diagrams are connected. The number 2 separated by a bar (|) from the condition specifies the relative frequency how often the switch condition is going to be checked.

Though the simple example seems to be manageable from a developer's perspective, Figure 9 corroborates that this is not the case any longer in a slightly more complex example: a TDL program with three modes and several input and output signal lines. Note that this is still the simplified modeling view the developer has. Even the usage of Multiplexer/Demultiplexer blocks and GoTo blocks does not help to simplify the model.

Benefits and Drawbacks. If modeling TDL programs without mode switching, the presented approach would be the most straightforward one. A Simulink user can easily accomplish that. It leads to better structured Simulink models where the timing and functionality behavior is separated. However, if modes are required, which typically is the case in practice, the model becomes too cluttered and thus barely understandable. In addition, the developer has to obey to several guidelines and naming conventions. The Simulink model editor does not provide means to give feedback about modeling rule violations. Potential violations could only be caught by the S/TDL translator tool when the model is processed. All the disadvantages of this approach compared to the separate TDL editor suite are discussed in section 3.2.

3   Separate TDL Editor Suite with Simulink as Simulation Platform

Analogous to the fact that StateFlow is a separate editor focused on state transition diagrams and integrated in the Simulink tool suite, a separate TDL editor suite can best support the developer in modeling the timing behavior of an application. Similar to StateFlow, the TDL Editor suite is well integrated to Simulink so that it seems to the user as if he or she would work with the same application.

The seamless integration, however, does not stop at providing a separate editor suite for modeling TDL applications: As mentioned before, execution times associated with all computation and communication activities are fixed and determined by the TDL program not by the platform. This means that TDL applications are platform-independent. To ensure that the timing behavior of such an application is the same on different platforms, a virtual machine called E machine is used. For supporting a new platform, only the E machine has to be ported to that platform. This section shows that it is possible to provide such an E machine for the Simulink simulation environment too. As a consequence of that fact, Simulink is not longer seen as a Simulation environment with some special treatment regarding the TDL toolchain. Indeed, Simulink is seen now as a platform like any other (hardware) platform. The section describes the new tool chain with the TDL editor suite and the Simulink platform from the developer's perspective. The enhanced throttle control case study, that now comprises two modes, illustrates the modeling of a sample application. A discussion of the advantages of this integration solution rounds out the paper.

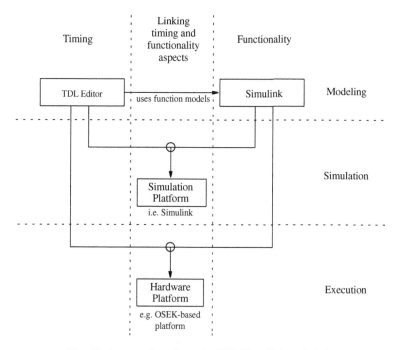

Fig. 10. An overview about the TDL/Simulink tool chain

3.1   The Tool Chain with the TDL Editor Suite

Figure 10 shows schematically how the tools interact. The TDL editor suite offers the developer a convenient development environment that is adjusted to the needs of TDL, without sacrificing the advantages of Simulink for modeling the functionality (control laws) and for modeling the plant that interacts with the TDL program (controller) during the simulation. The main aspects of the tool chain are separated by vertical dotted lines into the following three areas:

1. Description of the timing aspects of a control system corresponding to a TDL program
2. Implementation of the functionality (control laws) of a control system using Simulink
3. Linking of the timing and the functionality parts of the control system

In addition, Simulink is also used for modeling the plant by the use of standard Simulink blocks. The horizontal lines separate the development process into the modeling and simulation phase on a simulation platform (i.e. Simulink) as well as the execution phase on a specific hardware platform (e.g. OSEK based platforms). In the following, we discuss the three modeling and development steps in more detail.

TDL-Based Visual and Interactive Modeling: Separation of Timing and Functionality. The functionality, that is the implementation of the TDL tasks, is modeled in Simulink with the available Simulink blocks. The functionality, for example, a PID controller, is then provided as a Simulink subsystem, which can be easily accessed by the TDL editor suite.

The definition of the timing behavior and of the time-triggered mode switches is accomplished with the TDL editor suite. The TDL editor suite is a collection of the following tightly coupled editors:

1. *Mode transition editor:* This editor is used to specify when to switch between modes.
2. *Mode editor:* This editor allows the definition of a mode, that is, which TDL tasks it contains, how they interact, and how they communicate with sensors and actuators. The developer specifies which Simulink models are used for providing the functionality of the tasks.
3. *Mode communication editor:* The developer defines how values are copied between modes if a mode switch occurs.

In the following, we illustrate how the different editor types are used to define a TDL program according to our needs in the throttle control case study:

Defining the Control System in Simulink. A TDL program usually consists of one or more TDL modules. A TDL module defines a namespace for a set of TDL language constructs like modes, tasks, etc. In case of a distributed application, a TDL module is the smallest, undividable unit running on one processing node whereas several modules can run on one node. Independently if modules run on the same node or not, one module can import another module, which means that is has access to the imported module's sensors, task output ports, etc.

Regarding our case study, we define a Simulink model that is based on one TDL module. The model defines the interaction between the TDL module, that is, the controller, and the plant. This step is analogous to the one presented in Section 2.2 (see figure 4). The model consists of two blocks: One models the plant, which is a subsystem block that contains standard Simulink blocks. This block is connected to the TDL module block, which is provided by a TDL block library. In contrast to the model in Section 2.2, this block is not configured by mask variables or inner blocks provided by the TDL block library. A double-click opens an editor window of the TDL editor suite. The editor window consists of a left part (called the module navigator) and a right part that consists of one of the three editors listed above. If a new editor window opens, the right pane consists of the *mode transition editor* by default. The module navigator, which lists and organizes all types of TDL language constructs by using a tree representation, is used to navigate through the TDL module: Clicking on certain nodes of the navigator opens either a dialog to configure one concrete instance of a TDL language construct (e.g. a sensor) or displays an adequate editor within the right pane of the window (e.g. the mode editor regarding task assignment for a certain mode). The following paragraphs explain which editor is used to define what TDL language construct. From the developer's point of view, using the TDL editor suite is like opening the content of the TDL module block, which is modeled by using special editors.

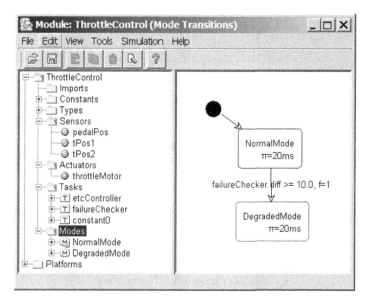

Fig. 11. Specification of mode switches

The Mode Transition Editor. In our example, the throttle control system can be in two modes, in the normal operation mode and in a failure mode. Figure 11 shows how the transition between the two modes is modeled by using the mode transition editor. As mentioned before, this editor is selected by default, if a new editor window opens. Alternatively, the mode transition editor (once the editor window has been opened already) is activated by clicking on the module node (i.e. the root node with the label ThrottleControl) or on the node with the label Modes, which organizes all defined modes of the module. The editor mimics a state diagram editor and does not allow the nesting of states. The NormalMode is marked as the start mode. The directed line connecting the NormalMode with the DegradedMode denotes that a mode switch occurs from the NormalMode to the DegradedMode if the mode switch condition becomes true. There is no connection between the modes in the other direction. This means that if the mode DegradedMode is entered, the TDL program cannot switch back into NormalMode until the program is restarted. The switch condition [failureChecker.diff ≥ 10] means that a mode switch occurs if the value of the task output port diff of the task failureChecker is greater or equal to 10. The task failureChecker calculates the difference of two measurements of the angle of the throttle.

The Mode Editor. This editor is opened by a single-click on one of the mode nodes of the module navigator (e.g. NormalMode). It allows the specification of TDL tasks and how they are connected to each other as well as to sensors and actuators (see Figure 12). The figure shows that NormalMode consists of two task blocks. The functionality of both tasks has been modeled in Simulink. As can be seen in the module navigator tree, every task consists of a task function too. This is indicated by a

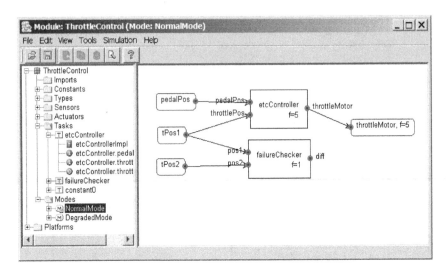

Fig. 12. The content of NormalMode

separate subnode of the task node that has a small rectangle containing the letter 'f' as its icon (e.g. the node etcControllerImpl). A double click on this node opens a new standard Simulink editor that shows the task functionality modeled by standard Simulink blocks. In this way, the TDL editor suite is seamlessly integrated into the Simulink environment.

The task function of the TDL task etcController is the same controller as the one presented in the previous sections. The task function of the task failureChecker calculates the difference between the two measurements of the throttle position. The tasks are connected to the corresponding sensors and actuators.

The DegradedMode contains only a task called constant0. The task has no input parameters and the output value of this task is constantly set to 0. Therefore, the throttle will be closed upon activation of this mode.

The Mode Communication Editor. Finally, we have to define how values are copied from one mode to another during a mode switch. Both mode input and mode output ports are a subset of the task output ports of the tasks contained in a mode. The mode communication editor (see figure 13) is opened either by a double-click on a connection line in the mode transition editor or by a single-click on the mode switch node found as a subnode of a mode node. In the case study, the output value of the task etcController should go to the output port of task constant0, though this has no effect on the behavior of the DegradedMode.

Simulink as Simulation Platform. TDL modules are typically developed as follows: First, a TDL module is defined either textually (TDL code) or graphically (using the TDL editor suite). The implementation of the task function (functionality code) is external to TDL and done in any imperative programming language. In case of using

tors (default Simulink editor and StateFlow editor) and intertwine the data flow between modes in case of mode switches (mode communication) with the data flow from the sensors and to the actuators. The dilemma is that this leads to diagrams that are difficult to understand. The best solution is a further editor together with the automatic update as provided by the separate TDL editor suite.

The necessity of introducing Merge blocks is one detail that further increases the complexity of the visual representation of the TDL-in-Simulink approach: two different source modes may copy to the same mode port of their common target mode. In the TDL editor suite, we model mode communication separately for each mode switch.

During a mode switch, values are copied between mode ports. Only task output ports can become mode ports. But in Simulink, it is not possible to connect two output ports. As a consequence, in the TDL-in-Simulink approach we have to connect output ports of the source mode block with Simulink input ports of the target mode block (by using the De/Multiplexer and Goto/From blocks; see Figure 9), though the input ports are semantically output ports. The 'input ports' are not used inside the mode block. They are only used for the specification of the model. This is, of course, extremely difficult to understand and a nightmare from the human-computer-interaction point of view. In contrast, in the TDL editor suite we simply connect the mode ports directly in the separate mode communication editor.

Finally, the Simulink editor is not TDL-syntax-sensitive so that no feedback can be provided if some aspects of the edited model are not correct. Only the S/TDL translator can detect errors in the model. This reduces the interactivity of the modeling process.

4 Conclusion

Overall, the combination of TDL and Simulink has several benefits. As TDL allows the time-safe, deterministic distribution of TDL components [9], the developer can easily come up with control systems that exhibit these properties that state-of-the-art tools do not support directly. In other words, the TDL component architecture frees the developer from targeting a specific single-node or distributed platform. He or she can focus on the application aspects, in particular the control problems. Furthermore, the resulting model is well structured into the timing and the functionality behavior.

The integration of TDL and Simulink modeling provides a powerful simulation environment. In addition, the TDL editor suite is fully integrated into the Simulink environment and is even designed to imitate Simulink's look and feel as far as possible. Experienced Simulink developers should grasp the combination with TDL quickly. In other words, the learning curve for experienced Simulink developers is supposed to be flat.

Acknowledgements

We thank Christoph Kirsch for his active support of the research described in this paper. He provided many useful hints for integrating Giotto and later TDL with Simulink as well as for the throttle control case study. Sebastian Fischmeister and Guido

Menkhaus helped us to investigate the integration of TDL modes in the transformation-based approach. Andreas Werner has suggested ideas for the design and has implemented large parts of the TDL editor suite. Finally, we thank Gerd Dauenhauer for his work regarding the implementation of the E machine for the Simulink simulation environment.

This research was supported in part by the FIT-IT Embedded Systems grant 807144 provided by the Austrian government through the 'Bundesminsterium für Verkehr, Innovation und Technologie'.

References

[1] Thomas A. Henzinger, Benjamin Horowitz, and Christoph Meyer Kirsch. Giotto: A Time-Triggered Language for Embedded Programming. Lecture Notes in Computer Science, 2211:166-184, 2001.

[2] Thomas A. Henzinger, Christoph M. Kirsch, Wolfgang Pree, and Marco A. A. Sanvido. From Control Models to Real-Time Code using Giotto. *IEEE Control Systems Magazine*, 23(1):50–64, February 2003.

[3] B. Horowitz, J. Liebman, C. Ma, T. John Koo, A. Sangiovanni-Vincentelli, and S. Sastry. Platform-Based Embedded Software Design and System Integration for Autonomous Vehicles. *IEEE Transactions*, 91(1):100 – 111, 2003.

[4] Christoph M. Kirsch. Principles of Real-Time Programming. *LNCS*, 2491, 2002.

[5] Hermann Kopetz and Gunther Bauer. The Time-Triggered Architecture. *IEEE Special Issue on Modeling and Design of Embedded Software*, 23(1), 2002.

[6] Edward A. Lee, Stephan Neuendorfer, and Michael J. Wirthlin. Actor-oriented design of embedded hardware and software systems. *Journal of Circuits, Systems, and Computers*, 12(3):231 – 260, 2003.

[7] Gerald Stieglbauer. Model-based Development of Embedded Control Systems with Giotto and Simulink. Master thesis, University of Salzburg, April 2003.

[8] Josef Templ. TDL Specification and Report. Technical report, Software Research Lab, University of Salzburg, Austria, October 2003.
http://www.SoftwareResearch.net/site/publications/C055.pdf

[9] Wolfgang Pree and Josef Templ. Towards a Component Architecture for Hard Real Time Control Applications, Automotive Software Workshop, San Diego, CA 10-12 January 2004.

[10] Thomas A. Henzinger, Christoph M. Kirsch, Slobodan Matic: Schedule Carrying Code, EmSoft03 conference, Philadelphia, PA, October 2003

[11] Gerd Dauenhauer. Simulink as a Simulation Platform for TDL. Technical Report, Software Research Lab, University of Salzburg, Austria, September 2005
http://www.SoftwareResearch.net/site/publications/T017.pdf

Author Index

Lecture Notes in Computer Science

For information about Vols. 1–4128

please contact your bookseller or Springer

Vol. 4178: A. Corradini, H. Ehrig, U. Montanari, L. Ribeiro, G. Rozenberg (Eds.), Graph Transformations. XII, 473 pages. 2006.

Vol. 4176: S.K. Katsikas, J. Lopez, M. Backes, S. Gritzalis, B. Preneel (Eds.), Information Security. XIV, 548 pages. 2006.

Vol. 4175: P. Bücher, B.M.E. Moret (Eds.), Algorithms in Bioinformatics. XII, 402 pages. 2006. (Sublibrary LNBI).

Vol. 4174: K. Franke, K.-R. Müller, B. Nickolay, R. Schäfer (Eds.), Pattern Recognition. XX, 773 pages. 2006.

Vol. 4173: S. El Yacoubi, B. Chopard, S. Bandini (Eds.), Cellular Automata. XV, 734 pages. 2006.

Vol. 4172: J. Gonzalo, C. Thanos, M. F. Verdejo, R.C. Carrasco (Eds.), Research and Advanced Technology for Digital Libraries. XVII, 569 pages. 2006.

Vol. 4169: H.L. Bodlaender, M.A. Langston (Eds.), Parameterized and Exact Computation. XI, 279 pages. 2006.

Vol. 4168: Y. Azar, T. Erlebach (Eds.), Algorithms – ESA 2006. XVIII, 843 pages. 2006.

Vol. 4167: S. Dolev (Ed.), Distributed Computing. XV, 576 pages. 2006.

Vol. 4166: J. Górski (Ed.), Computer Safety, Reliability, and Security. XIV, 440 pages. 2006.

Vol. 4165: W. Jonker, M. Petković (Eds.), Secure, Data Management. X, 185 pages. 2006.

Vol. 4163: H. Bersini, J. Carneiro (Eds.), Artificial Immune Systems. XII, 460 pages. 2006.

Vol. 4162: R. Královič, P. Urzyczyn (Eds.), Mathematical Foundations of Computer Science 2006. XV, 814 pages. 2006.

Vol. 4161: R. Harper, M. Rauterberg, M. Combetto (Eds.), Entertainment Computing - ICEC 2006. XXVII, 417 pages. 2006.

Vol. 4160: M. Fisher, W.v.d. Hoek, B. Konev, A. Lisitsa (Eds.), Logics in Artificial Intelligence. XII, 516 pages. 2006. (Sublibrary LNAI).

Vol. 4159: J. Ma, H. Jin, L.T. Yang, J.J.-P. Tsai (Eds.), Ubiquitous Intelligence and Computing. XXII, 1190 pages. 2006.

Vol. 4158: L.T. Yang, H. Jin, J. Ma, T. Ungerer (Eds.), Autonomic and Trusted Computing. XIV, 613 pages. 2006.

Vol. 4156: S. Amer-Yahia, Z. Bellahsène, E. Hunt, R. Unland, J.X. Yu (Eds.), Database and XML Technologies. IX, 123 pages. 2006.

Vol. 4155: O. Stock, M. Schaerf (Eds.), Reasoning, Action and Interaction in AI Theories and Systems. XVIII, 343 pages. 2006. (Sublibrary LNAI).

Vol. 4154: Y.A. Dimitriadis, I. Zigurs, E. Gómez-Sánchez (Eds.), Groupware: Design, Implementation, and Use. XIV, 438 pages. 2006.

Vol. 4153: N. Zheng, X. Jiang, X. Lan (Eds.), Advances in Machine Vision, Image Processing, and Pattern Analysis. XIII, 506 pages. 2006.

Vol. 4152: Y. Manolopoulos, J. Pokorný, T. Sellis (Eds.), Advances in Databases and Information Systems. XV, 448 pages. 2006.

Vol. 4151: A. Iglesias, N. Takayama (Eds.), Mathematical Software - ICMS 2006. XVII, 452 pages. 2006.

Vol. 4150: M. Dorigo, L.M. Gambardella, M. Birattari, A. Martinoli, R. Poli, T. Stützle (Eds.), Ant Colony Optimization and Swarm Intelligence. XVI, 526 pages. 2006.

Vol. 4149: M. Klusch, M. Rovatsos, T.R. Payne (Eds.), Cooperative Information Agents X. XII, 477 pages. 2006. (Sublibrary LNAI).

Vol. 4148: J. Vounckx, N. Azemard, P. Maurine (Eds.), Integrated Circuit and System Design. XVI, 677 pages. 2006.

Vol. 4147: M. Broy, I.H. Krüger, M. Meisinger (Eds.), Automotive Software – Connected Services in Mobile Networks. XIV, 155 pages. 2006.

Vol. 4146: J.C. Rajapakse, L. Wong, R. Acharya (Eds.), Pattern Recognition in Bioinformatics. XIV, 186 pages. 2006. (Sublibrary LNBI).

Vol. 4144: T. Ball, R.B. Jones (Eds.), Computer Aided Verification. XV, 564 pages. 2006.

Vol. 4143: R. Lämmel, J. Saraiva, J. Visser (Eds.), Generative and Transformational Techniques in Software Engineering. X, 471 pages. 2006.

Vol. 4142: A. Campilho, M. Kamel (Eds.), Image Analysis and Recognition, Part II. XXVII, 923 pages. 2006.

Vol. 4141: A. Campilho, M. Kamel (Eds.), Image Analysis and Recognition, Part I. XXVIII, 939 pages. 2006.

Vol. 4139: T. Salakoski, F. Ginter, S. Pyysalo, T. Pahikkala, Advances in Natural Language Processing. XVI, 771 pages. 2006. (Sublibrary LNAI).

Vol. 4138: X. Cheng, W. Li, T. Znati (Eds.), Wireless Algorithms, Systems, and Applications. XVI, 709 pages. 2006.

Vol. 4137: C. Baier, H. Hermanns (Eds.), CONCUR 2006 – Concurrency Theory. XIII, 525 pages. 2006.

Vol. 4136: R.A. Schmidt (Ed.), Relations and Kleene Algebra in Computer Science. XI, 433 pages. 2006.

Vol. 4135: C.S. Calude, M.J. Dinneen, G. Păun, G. Rozenberg, S. Stepney (Eds.), Unconventional Computation. X, 267 pages. 2006.

Vol. 4134: K. Yi (Ed.), Static Analysis. XIII, 443 pages. 2006.

Vol. 4133: J. Gratch, M. Young, R. Aylett, D. Ballin, P. Olivier (Eds.), Intelligent Virtual Agents. XIV, 472 pages. 2006. (Sublibrary LNAI).

Vol. 4132: S. Kollias, A. Stafylopatis, W. Duch, E. Oja (Eds.), Artificial Neural Networks – ICANN 2006, Part II. XXXIV, 1028 pages. 2006.

Vol. 4131: S. Kollias, A. Stafylopatis, W. Duch, E. Oja (Eds.), Artificial Neural Networks – ICANN 2006, Part I. XXXIV, 1008 pages. 2006.

Vol. 4130: U. Furbach, N. Shankar (Eds.), Automated Reasoning. XV, 680 pages. 2006. (Sublibrary LNAI).

Vol. 4129: D. McGookin, S. Brewster (Eds.), Haptic and Audio Interaction Design. XII, 167 pages. 2006.